ARKANA

CHRISTIANITY
AND YOGA

Dr Justin O'Brien is a stress management consultant and Director of Education at Marylebone Health Centre, London. He was formerly a Professor of Religious Studies and East/West Philosophy at Loyola University, Chicago, Illinois, and the Himalayan International Institute. He has lived and trained in the Christian monasteries of Europe, the ashrams of India, the zendos of Japan, and other holy places around the world. He lectures internationally on the synthesis between Eastern spiritual understanding and Christianity.

JUSTIN O'BRIEN

CHRISTIANITY
AND YOGA

A MEETING OF MYSTIC PATHS

ARKANA

ARKANA

Published by the Penguin Group
27 Wrights Lane, London W8 5TZ, England
Viking Penguin Inc., 40 West 23rd Street, New York,
New York 10010, USA
Penguin Books Australia Ltd, Ringwood, Victoria, Australia
Penguin Books Canada Ltd, 2801 John Street, Markham, Ontario,
Canada L3R 1B4
Penguin Books (NZ) Ltd, 182–190 Wairau Road, Auckland 10,
New Zealand

Penguin Books Ltd, Registered Offices; Harmondsworth, Middlesex,
England

First published in Great Britain by Arkana 1989

Filmset in 10 on 12½ point Bembo by Input Typesetting Ltd, London

Printed in Great Britain by Guernsey Press Co. Ltd.,
Guernsey, Channel Islands

A CIP catalogue record for this book is available from the
British Library

To Theresa
whose heart knows
the meaning of nurturing

Contents

Foreword

Several years ago Swami Rama of the Himalayas remarked to me, "One of the beautiful gems of Christian tradition is found in the words of Jesus where he said, 'No one comes to the Father but by me' " (John 14:6). "Unfortunately," he continued, "it appears that possibly half of Christendom takes this to mean that anyone who isn't baptized and a practicing Christian is excluded from communion with God, while it seems about as many more speak apologetically as if either Jesus had been misreported or made an audacious claim he had no business making. But we see that his claim was to Christ Consciousness or consciousness of the true Self which is divine. Jesus Christ had every right to say what he is reported to have said. And while our terminology may differ, we also say, 'there is no other way to God.' "

I concurred. Yet thinking back over my life, especially to the years spent in training and preparation for the vocation and ministry of an Episcopal priest, I recalled the time when Swami Rama's sage observation and witness, at the very least, would have caught me by surprise. Surely my paramount question would have been, how could one who practices a spirituality which isn't even regarded as religion, let alone Christian religion, seriously make such a Christian affirmation? Would I have welcomed the state of puzzlement into which he would have thrown me? The counsel of Jesus to his disciples might have come to my aid: "Whoever is not against us is for us" (Luke 9:50; Mark 9:40). My youthful zeal to disavow any claim to truth which sounded as if it hadn't derived from the Bible

might likewise have been dealt a healthy blow by the magnanimous insight of the apostle John: "Whoever is a loving person
has been born of God and knows God" (1 John 4:7).

So I mused and mused again. Could I, likewise, twenty-five
years ago, have appreciated as readily and thankfully as I do
today the offering presented in Dr Justin O'Brien's splendid
book, *Christianity and Yoga: A Meeting of Mystic Paths*? Would
the sound of the book's title alone have struck me as suspect?
You, no doubt, have pondered its title, read its table of contents
and allowed its logo (two candles generating a single flame) to
register in your mind. Now you may wonder whether or not
you're really looking for what it may have to offer. Or, perhaps,
with more or less than I of living, searching, wrestling and
practicing on the spiritual journey, already you have come to
anticipate the important contribution this work may prove itself
to be. Either way, I believe, a wealth of insight awaits you as
you read.

Jesus taught, "Behold the Kingdom of God is within you . . .
like a treasure hidden in a field!" (Luke 17:21; Matthew 13:44).
Socrates (in Plato's *Phaedrus*) says, "I must first know myself,
as the Delphinian inscription says. To be curious about that
which is not my concern, while I am still in ignorance of my
own self, would be ridiculous." Dr O'Brien has long taken such
counsels to heart and made of them a living practice.

Perhaps you too glory in the name Christian but are of the
inclusive and not the exclusive kind. If so, you meet in Justin
O'Brien a strong companion in the Way. He is richly qualified
to write with authority about yoga and Christianity – about the
Single Flame. Thus a rich fare awaits the reader. Let us speak a
word of blessing and savor the feast!

Ralph C. Roth, M.Div.
Trinity Church
Mount Pocono, Pennsylvania

Foreword

This book builds bridges between the great tradition of Christianity and the science of yoga. The word yoga is much misunderstood in the Western hemisphere – some see yoga as a fad, and others as a kind of religion. Actually yoga is a systematic science, a set of techniques, and while yoga itself is not a religion, its practical teachings are an integral part of the great religions of the world. The Book of Genesis, the Sermon on the Mount, and the Book of Revelations all contain yogic teachings, and in the Psalms there are numerous references to the yogic method of meditation.

The origins of yoga are obscure and go back many thousands of years. Its central teaching is that man's essential nature is divine, perfect, and infinite. He remains unaware of this reality, however, because he constantly identifies himself with his body, mind, and external objects. That false identification makes him think and feel that he is imperfect and limited, subject to sorrow, death, and decay. Comparing the science of yoga with the great religions of the world, particularly Christianity, one realizes that yoga science offers practical methods to aspirants of any religion, so that they can know the center of consciousness within. Through the meditative methods of yoga one can dispel the darkness of ignorance, and become aware of his essential nature, which is free from all imperfections.

The author of this book, Dr Justin O'Brien, is eminently qualified to write about both the yogic tradition and Christianity. He has been a respected teacher of philosophy and theology for twenty-five years, and a serious student of yoga for nearly twenty years. His work creates a bridge to greater understanding on the part of the Westerners for the practical utility of the yogic techniques so that they can enhance the spiritual growth and transformation of Christians and deepen their own rich tradition.

Swami Rama
Founder and Spiritual Head,
Himalayan International Institute
of Yoga Science and Philosophy

Preface

The breadth of diversity in Christian spirituality startles even Christians. A careful examination of Christianity over the centuries demonstrates that Christian spirituality is not a single thread any more than Christian faith is one exclusive denomination. Spirituality is like a tapestry requiring many dyed threads woven together to form a masterpiece.

Likewise, those rituals and ceremonies that play an important part in the Christian churches have a long, ennobling history influenced by many diverse elements. For example, the Catholic Mass, like the Jewish Seder, features a sacred meal, which itself is common to many ancient religious rites. The use of incense, candles, food, fire, bodily gestures, and special garments in Christian liturgical occasions, although varied in style, trace their origin to ancient Eastern ritual. The underlying unity in these items is their appreciation as sacred things, that is, something sacramental. Among the sacred things of the world, Christians accord precedence to human beings, for they are the image and likeness of God.

Knowledge of the complexities of human nature is not the prerogative of one science any more than Christian values belong exclusively to one church. This human nature that bears a sacred imprint displays a versatility expressed over the centuries in many cultures. History is one long drama depicting how peoples acknowledge or resent their nature and destiny.

In my travels in the East and West I have been fortunate to meet and experience some of today's episodes in this ongoing drama. What caught my interest were the recurring questions that citizens of many countries raised about the benefits and deficiencies that they sensed in their customary forms and practices of spirituality. There were many who doubted and resented the Christian influences of their upbringing. There were those who sensed that Christian values are richer than their best presentation by an institutional church. There were those who suspected that Christianity may have benefits yet to be discovered by man's search for the meaning of life.

From exposure to these questionings over the years, this series of essays took shape. To all these attitudes I have attempted to bring a rich tradition from the Himalayas. The science of yoga displays a perspective on human nature that may astonish in its optimism. By contrasting and comparing both traditions, I hope to provoke readers to look at Christianity from a new perspective and encourage dialogue from a sense of the truth of both. In this reflection and experimentation modern man can thus be aided in his quest for spiritual fulfilment.

JOB

CHAPTER 1

Traditions In Tandem

In the second century, St Justin Martyr said, "Whatever has been nobly spoken in any place is a part of Christian heritage."[1] The winds of history blow a new climate in today's Christianity as it carries forward the words of the past. In these final years of the twentieth century, traditional Western approaches to religious thought and spirituality are undergoing revision. We are recognizing those nobly spoken words from many places that have long inspired fellow seekers. We are learning that genuine spirituality exists in many guises. We are admitting that pluralism in approaches does not endanger one's preferred beliefs nor reduce traditions to meaningless equality. Rather we are expanding, as St Justin advised, our Christian heritage.

The Vatican's recognition of the importance of other traditions was proclaimed by Archbishop Jean Jadot in a recent bulletin:

> . . . we are now far more vividly aware that several religious traditions such as the Hindu and the Buddhist and the Chinese traditions point to rich fonts of spirituality which they describe as 'sacred or holy literature,' their 'holy books'. . . . If such writings are part of mankind's spiritual heritage, should we not learn how to read them intelligently? Could they not be a help for us to gain new insights and deepen our appreciation of our own Christian traditions?[2]

These statements characterize the new wind affecting mutual

consideration among traditions. People are less fearsome in noticing truth preserved in other traditions. Similarly, the scientific comprehension of human nature, notably in the area of neuropsychology, has undergone drastic revisions. Medical schools, for example, no longer teach that human volition cannot affect the autonomic nervous system. On the contrary, experimental evidence has thoroughly demonstrated that the human mind can duly influence any region of the body. While these ideas seem new in our culture, the broad acknowledgement of mind over matter has always been a basic tenet of the ancient science of yoga.

An understanding of human nature is essential to spiritual growth and transformation. Theologically speaking, it is a common principle that creation is a revelation to mankind of the meaning of God. Since Genesis singles out men and women as the image and likeness of divinity, it would be reasonable to expect that the more one knows about human nature, individually and collectively, the more one could fathom the ultimate source of reality.

To this extent, yoga, while not a religion, presents to followers of any religion an opportunity for systematic growth in self-knowledge. Yoga belongs to the wisdom heritage of mankind. Its purpose is not merely physical health and suppleness nor peace of mind, though these are benefits of yoga practice. Yoga's goal is to aid people in understanding themselves as completely as possible. Yoga does not attempt to supply the answers to modern-day problems, but shows people how to deal with themselves in terms of discovering their native endowment. Christians would, no doubt, appreciate a tradition that improves one's well-being and encourages the enrichment of their society.

Since yoga traces its many branches to ancient wisdom, it is not surprising that some of its insight into human nature has been incorporated into religion and culture over the centuries. Many of the hygienic practices for sound health that are a part of the contemporary scene, for example, are found in yoga manuals composed hundreds of years ago. Likewise, some of the main ideas of yoga now becoming familiar in the West are discernible in many walks of life.

The Path of Worship

When Christians gather together for religious services they are performing worship. In examining the 400 versions of Christianity in the Western hemisphere, it is evident that very few of them dispense with worship. Christians need to be reminded that liturgy is not unique to Christianity but is a universal action performed in ancient as well as modern times.

Worship (or *puja*, as it is called in the ancient *Vedas*), has always been viewed as a form for achieving the highest freedom. Some Christians narrow their acts of worship to a compulsion based on fear as if they were approaching a stern God who demands weekly compliance with His* laws. Their motive resembles that of a debtor paying his just dues. But a reading of the words of Christ at the last supper within the entire context of John's Gospel reveals a very different interpretation. Here the meaning of worship approaches a recognition of participation in an action that leads to human liberation. Worship becomes a way to immortality. Those in community are joined with the divine through special acts.

Without knowing it, in their highest cultic acts Christians are practicing an ancient form of yoga. They are practicing *bhakti* yoga. This is not a thin label pointing to surface similarities. Genuine worship is more than paying a debt or uttering prayers; it is an action that aims at banishing the duality of everyday living. This is the same as the definition of *bhakti* yoga which is a way of offering oneself totally to the divine and uniting with it through devotion and reverence.

* While asserting that God is genderless, the author's use of the male gender in its application to the divine throughout this book is simply following conventional usage for ease of reading.

In worship man unites himself reverentially to God. This is the meaning of sacrifice – to make one holy. The worshiping community joins together to become joined to the divine. The visible act of joining to the divine life is enacted especially at the time of communion.

This symbolism is vividly portrayed in the Bible. Just as creation is God's sacrifice (for He brings it into being, preserves it, and allows it to renew itself) so now through man's act of worship the universe returns itself to its divine origin for renewal. In this way, worship reminds man that he can escape the humdrum – *samsara* – and be reunited with his true destiny. He celebrates existence by coming into loving contact with the source of existence. This devotional joining of man with the divine unites and renews, thus qualifying as a form of yoga, which means "to yoke or unite." In this way the Christian liturgy reveals a basic aspiration in its followers and joins a long line of traditions which have recognized the need for immortality.

The Path of Action

Many Christians are involved in professional and domestic actions that fulfill their talents as well as pay the bills. Often these actions are performed primarily for the good of those who will benefit from them. Both the intention and the consequent actions stemming from the intention are directed towards the benefit of those who receive the action. In every community one can recognize people who are especially noted for being reliable, honest and competent in their jobs. Equally important one usually finds these same characteristics demonstrated by parents in their loving concern for their families. In this way Christians of every denomination practice a form of yoga called *karma-marga*.

Christians who expend themselves unselfishly for others, who recognize the value of excellence in their professional relations, who skillfully interact with peers and who foster friendships with others are developing spiritually through the practice of *karma* yoga as they develop Christian virtue. In *karma* yoga one speaks of doing actions unselfishly, giving up the fruits or results to the intended person. In Christian circles, one speaks of developing virtues, especially charity, whereby one serves the other person without concern for reward. This splendid human attitude of respectful service for others is universally recognized as a basic step on the path to full spiritual maturity.

The Path of Knowledge

The names of Tillich, Rahner, Zaehner, Lossky, James, Hocking, Marechal, Lonergan and many others depict individuals who sought to grasp the intelligibility of the absolute. They were practicing *jnana* yoga. Like the Church Fathers and medieval philosopher/theologians, these writers expressed their pursuit of the absolute under the inspiration of truth.

Whereas devotion and service have characterized the first two examples of Christians practicing yoga, this path of human development reveals the conscious effort to understand the ultimate as far as it is possible. The pursuit of truth has led scientists, artists, writers and philosophers on an adventure in knowledge where gradually they have learned to discern reality from appearance.

The power of the mind has the ability to live from the truth that one has experienced. The love for truth can become the basis for a way of life that has enthralled men and women from every age. Serious Christians desire to know themselves, thus echoing an aspiration that is earlier than the writing of the Bible. Self-knowledge is a profound necessity. Without it man can hardly hope to fathom the practicalities of life, let alone its ultimate meaning.

Hardly anyone would refuse to become wise. Yet only a few, Christian or otherwise, have labored on behalf of wisdom. The knowledge called wisdom is a knowledge which comes through experiencing the highest truth.

Genuine philosophers, theologians and scientists are never satisfied with merely an intellectual familiarity with the world. They are induced by the pursuit of truth to exceed the senses and rational mind. Thus they move from *apara vidya* (ordinary science) to *para vidya* (the science of the absolute). In this science one experiences the truth directly. Christian faith can then spur one on to seek the direct experience of the absolute as far as his capacities can take him. Hence the compatibility of the Christian allegiance to the pursuing of highest truth in the path of *jnana* yoga, the way of realized wisdom.

The Royal Path

While Christian mystics seem a strange lot and legends and stories describe their lives as a series of incredible adventures, they are actually the most balanced of people, for they have involved their entire being in the pursuit of total fulfillment. Similar in approach is the broad path of *astanga* yoga, known more popularly as *raja* yoga – the royal route. This path is for someone who enjoys a holistic approach involving body, mind and spirit. The famous eight rungs or stages in *raja* yoga comprise an overall development of the individual personality. It is a path that combines theory with practice.

In reading the works of St John of the Cross, for example, one finds an acute analysis of the mind, its faculties and its relationship to the body. The saint explains the adventure in higher consciousness by elaborating in detail the various movements, desires, imaginings and subconscious episodes that occur in spiritual growth. John shows that the spiritual undertaking has a rationale that, while not abstract or stifling to the spirit, nevertheless reveals a definite causal order in spiritual growth.

Likewise the major work of yoga, Patanjali's *Yoga Sutras*, reveals a map of consciousness that surprisingly concurs in many instances with John's program for spiritual realization. Both authors describe the human ascent from the grossest, sensual level to the subtlest, transcendental experiences that supersede rational awareness. Incorporated into the Sutras are the traditional threefold phases of purgation, illumination and union that are described in many Christian writings on spiritual development.

The principal activity that centers the lives of Christian mystics as well as *raja* yogis is meditation. More than any other exercise, both traditions look to meditation as the *sine qua non* for spiritual perfection. From the obvious yoga disciplines of the Desert Fathers to the renaissance of meditation today the Christian endorsement of meditation has a long and consistent history.

Then why does yoga and meditation seem to have come from the East and appear as something new for Christians? We live amidst cultural pressures. Sometimes the problems in society focus upon only certain aspects of a broad tradition. While every Christian tries to be charitable in their daily life, for example, it was not until this century that many Christians saw the incompatibility of treating some human beings as slaves. Only recently have theologians pointed out how some have distorted the gospels to make women suffer in subservience to men. History shows that each generation retains and loses some of its older wisdom.

Thus, meditation receded from the churches' consciousness and became a specialty for monks and nuns. The resurgence of interest in meditation in the churches today is a return to the crossroads where yoga and Christianity meet for the task of human perfection.

Conclusion

These paths of yoga – *bhakti, karma, jnana* and *raja* – are some of the various approaches that yoga science has developed for enabling people to understand the vast complexities of living. Through careful comparisons of yoga and Christianity one can recognize that the philosophy and practice of yoga will lead a

Christian to greater creativity as well as a deeper understanding of the human spirit and the riches of his religious tradition.

CHAPTER 2

The Ways of Religious Consciousness

Once upon a time there was a village situated in a valley near the Andes Mountains. The inhabitants had lived in this valley for many generations and grew to revere the awesome mountains with their snow peaks reaching into the heavens. On special days of the year the elders revealed to the people the sacredness of the mountains: it was these lofty peaks that brought the rainfall for the crops and protected them from all dangers. Seeing these distant peaks and remembering the consoling words, the villagers enjoyed a sense of security. The villagers showed their reverence to the mountains by bowing to them upon rising from sleep and before retiring at night.

One day some young people decided that they wanted to walk out of the valley and investigate the mountains at close range. They announced this to their astonished parents who immediately ran to the elders for advice. The elders were also shocked at the proposal. No one in their history had ever considered climbing the mountains! They sternly reminded the young ones that it was impossible to climb the mountains. The important truth for them to remember was that the mountains were not for climbing, but for revering. Besides, the range was too far away and the long journey would be fraught with unknown dangers. The entire village attempted to persuade the youngsters to change their minds, but to no avail. They were encouraged to be satisfied with the security of village life and the blessings which the mountains daily bestowed. To the eager young people, the journey through danger seemed only to point out the great value of the adventure. They thought the more they could explore the mountains, the more they would revere their beauty and purpose in their lives.

The young ones soon departed and began their struggle through the dense forests and severe weather of the mountains. The distance to their goal seemed longer and harder than antici-pated. At times they felt they should turn back, but always some inner longing kept them moving ahead. Finally, many weeks later, an exhausted party climbed onto a plateau over-looking the far side of the mountain range. There to their amaze-ment were sights unseen by any villager: vast meadows with clear, blue lakes; strange animals grazing among the fruits and berries of the slopes; miles of prairies rolling with wild flowers and grains. But most amazing of all, they were welcomed by people who lived in the peaks and who shared their knowledge of the land. A whole new world opened before them.

Eventually the young people returned down the mountains to their valley. They were anxious to tell the villagers their tales of the sacred mountains. To their utter surprise, they spoke to deaf ears; no one would believe them, for such things were impossible.

Just as there are two ways to approach the mountains in our story, so there are two ways to approach religious conscious-ness. In either instance, a reverential attitude toward the sacred is preserved, but the distance differs. Most people are inclined to tread the path of religious truth through faith. A few are inclined to search further than faith in hopes of finding concrete experiences that justify their search. This essay shall explore these two paths.

For the sake of clarification, we shall use distinct terms to show the difference of approach within religious consciousness. It is not a matter of separating believers from unbelievers. Taking the lead from the Judeo-Christian Bible, one notes that there is a division of teachings that are given to an initiatory group – the school of prophets in the Old Testament and the

disciples in the New Testament – while less revealing teachings
are given to the ordinary crowd of believers. Although this
division of teachings is found consistently throughout the Bible,
it is not unique to these scriptures. This twofold approach is
found throughout ancient scriptures. The New Testament
especially illustrates this division. Jesus speaks parables to the
ordinary believers while revealing the mystery or esoteric meanings to his specially chosen students.

> To you has been given the secret of the Kingdom of God,
> but for those outside everything is in parables; so that they
> may indeed see but not perceive, and may indeed hear but
> not understand. . . . (Mark 4:10)
> He would not speak to them except in parables, but he
> explained everything to his disciples when they were alone.
> (Mark 4:34)

This distinction in religious consciousness rests upon this scriptural insistence. Thus we have esoteric teachings and exoteric
teachings. Exoteric means suitable to be imparted to the public,
or to a less-initiated circle. Esoteric means knowledge that is
restricted to a small group, or understood by specially initiated
ones. So in the scriptures, there are exoteric teachings
presentable to the public and shared by ordinary believers.
Another set of teachings is available only to initiated followers.
These esoteric teachings are inaccessible to the sincere but ordinary believer.

The Exoteric Believers

The conventional exoteric approach to religious truth appeals
to the majority of modern Christians. They fill the registered
membership of the various denominations. Believers inclined
toward the exoteric dimension feel at home among the Bible,
the dogmas, beliefs and rituals. There is an emphasis on
communion and fellowship. There are ample sub-organizations

within the church structure to allow for social participation and expression of their practical faith. The church bulletin would list a whole gamut of social activities from fund drives and bake sales to scouting, volunteer hospital work and adult education classes. All these programs invite participation from the church membership. The worship services and social opportunities comprise a large network of religious symbols that unify the faith community. The primary interest of these believers is to support this symbol system that inspires and consolidates their faith. Belonging to a church, taking part in church-sponsored activities, reinforces the faith of the committed believer. Similar motivation would be found among Jewish membership in a synagogue.

The religious testimony of the believers obvious within the faith community and evident to the citizens of the larger, cultural community, demonstrates the exoteric plane of consciousness. While a believer acknowledges an ultimate source, usually under the term "God," he engenders his religious security and meaning by supporting the symbolic complex that elaborates his unique church affiliation. The Baptist has one way, the Quaker another. The symbols of a preferred denomination – the church's beliefs and activities – define for the believer his attitude toward life's expectations. These believers, like the villagers in our story, live within the borders of their beliefs.

The Esoteric Believers

The esoteric believer usually, but not necessarily, starts his spiritual journey from an exoteric stance. He learned and adhered to the conventional beliefs of the denominational community. He envisaged, as far as his spiritual commitment was concerned, a religious destiny completely within the guidelines provided by church authorities and their interpretation of the Bible. Somewhere along his spiritual odyssey, the conventional believer was shaken to the roots of his beliefs. Unforeseen, and certainly unexpected, his religious orientation was challenged: his cherished beliefs could not reply to the new questions arising from his life's experience.

This challenge often produces, in the mind and heart of the believer, a spiritual conflict. One wants to uphold his allegiance to his church beliefs and yet he cannot deny that his life experience does not seem to make sense on the basis of his beliefs. Sometimes this perplexing situation in the believer's mind results from a long chain of events, apparently unrelated, but having an accumulative impact upon his conventional beliefs. In rare instances, there is such a disruptive experience that the believer almost immediately reorients himself in light of the new event.

An exceptional conversion of this type is the story of Sundar Singh, who lived in the first part of this century. An Indian Sikh by birth and education, the young Sundar was the sworn enemy of Christ and all Christians. One evening, to his total surprise, he had a vision of Christ that so overwhelmed him that his basic honesty could not be unimpelled by the genuineness of the spiritual experience. Like St Paul, Sundar responded immediately to the implications of his vision. It brought such clarity of meaning in his life that he cast aside Sikh orthodoxy to accept Christian baptism. He spent the rest of his austere life playing out the continuing inspiration of his experience. It is interesting to note that while he accepted Christian baptism, he refused to align himself with any formal church. His Christian message to the world was constructed along the lines of a non-denominational portrait of Jesus Christ.

An earlier example would be the life of the eighteenth-century mystic, Emmanuel Swedenborg. Here was a brilliant scientist, scholar and political figure of Sweden who had been brought up in the orthodox Lutheran faith of his nation. He underwent a midlife crisis in his fifties in which his religious values were challenged by a series of dreams and visions that overthrew his exoteric faith. In pursuing the meaning of these experiences,

Swedenborg was led to reinterpret the significance of Christianity from a perspective based upon his meditational exploration of human consciousness. He remained a loyal church member for many years until an accidental discovery by his minister of his unorthodox beliefs led to his legal persecution.

Similarly, the esoteric believer, already an orthodox member of his faith community undergoes a startling experience that produces a new understanding. The knowledge derived from this experience vastly exceeds anything learned in the conventional beliefs. Consequently, the believer is no longer comfortable with the quality of knowledge that prevails for an exoteric believer. He may remain in the church membership, as did Emmanuel Swedenborg, or quietly depart, as did Sundar Singh. In either case the intelligibility of the experience impells him to revise his interpretation of life and destiny. His new knowledge does not necessarily annull his former beliefs but gives them a permanent grounding that removes spiritual doubt and provides correction where needed.

The following excerpts are descriptions of the esoteric consciousness. These are taken from the acclaimed writings of saints and sages from both the Christian and the yoga traditions.

Men who are inward and contemplative must go out,
according to the manner of contemplation, beyond reason
and beyond discretion; and beyond their created nature, with
an everlasting beholding in this inborn light, and so they
shall become transformed, and one with this same light by
which they see, and which they are. . . . For in this
contemplation . . . he remains free and master of himself in
inwardness and in virtue.

Jan van Ruysbroek (1293–1381)[1]

If I am to know God directly, I must become completely
He and He I; so that this He and this I become and are one I.

Meister Eckhart (1260–1329)[2]

Some may ask, what is it to be a partaker of the Divine
Nature or a godlike man? He who is imbued with or
illuminated by the Eternal or Divine Light and inflamed or
consumed with eternal or divine love, he is a deified man
and a partaker of the divine nature.

> Anonymous author of the fourteenth century Theologia
> Germanica[3]

I saw God! . . . I beheld a fullness and a clearness and felt
them within me so abundantly that I cannot describe it, or
give any likeness thereof. I cannot say I saw anything
corporeal. I beheld the ineffable fullness, but I can relate
nothing of it, save that I have seen in it the Sovereign Good.

> St Angela of Foligno (1248–1309)[4]

. . . how glorious is that soul who has indeed been able to
pass from the stormy ocean to Me, the sea pacific, and in
that sea, which is myself, the supreme and eternal Deity,
to fill the pitcher of her heart.

> St Catherine of Sienna (1347–1380)[5]

The divine dark is the inaccessible light where God is said
to dwell. Because transcendent clarity, it is invisible. Because
from the heights comes its light, it is inaccessible. All
worthy are they who enter there to know and to look upon
God. Unseeing and unknowing they attain in truth what
is beyond all seeing and all knowing.

> Dionysius, sixth century[6]

That mind is perfect which through true faith, in supreme
ignorance supremely knows the supremely knowable, and
which, in gazing upon the universe of his handiwork, has
received from God comprehensive knowledge of His
providence and judgment – but I speak after the manner
of men.

> St Maximus (580–662)[7]

Eye cannot see him, nor words reveal him. . . . When the
mind is cleansed by the grace of wisdom, he is seen by
contemplation, the One without parts.

Maitri Upanishad 6.17[8]

So the wise man, freed from name and form, attains the
Supreme divine Person.

Mandaka Upanishad 3.2.8[9]

The external which resides in the soul should be known.
Beyond this there is nothing that needs to be known. The
enjoyer, the object of enjoyment, the Inspirer – this has
been declared to be the All, the threefold Divinity.

Swetasvatara Upanishad 2.15[10]

Contemplating him who has neither beginning, middle nor
end, the One, the all-pervading, who is intellect and bliss,
the formless, the wonderful . . . the silent sage reaches the
source of Being, the universal witness, on the other shore
of darkness.

Kaivalya Upanishad 7[11]

A certain wise man, in search of immortality turned his
gaze inward and saw the divine self within.

Katha Upanishad 4.1[12]

Then Naciketas, instructed by Death, having embraced this
knowledge and the whole yoga discipline, passed over to
the divine and became free from stain and exempt from
death; and so too is anyone who possesses this knowledge
of the divine Self within himself.

Katha Upanishad 6.18[13]

The holy soul, when by the inward excitement of its fervor,
it is cut off from itself, when it is moved by ecstasy of mind

to rise up above itself, when it is carried away altogether and rests in a celestial world, when it is wholly immersed in angelic visions, seems to have transcended the limitations of its native powers.

Richard of St Victor (d. 1173)[14]

. . . in contemplation is for the soul to retreat within itself. The third step is for the soul to raise itself beyond itself and to strive to see two things: its creator and his own nature. But the soul can never attain to this until it has learned to subdue every image . . . to reject whatever may come to it through sight or hearing . . . or any bodily sensation, and to tread it down, so that the soul may see what it itself is outside of its body. After this . . . let your naked intention fly up above all human reasoning and there you shall find such great sweetness and such great secrets that without special grace there is no one who can think of it except only him who has experienced it.

St Edmund Rich (1180–1240)[15]

. . . those things which are known clearly about God and which are beheld by a mind made worthy by exceeding purity, are said to be the glory of God which is seen. So the mind, purified and passing beyond everything material, so that it perfects its contemplation of God, is made divine in what it contemplates.

Origen (185–253)[16]

From a simple reading of these descriptions from Western and Eastern sources, it seems quite obvious that these words could hardly be expressive of denominational beliefs nor conventional piety. If one were to examine a church charter, its prayer books and hymnals, nothing like these descriptions will be found. The meaning of these words connote a radical difference from the exoteric mentality.

All of the above Eastern quotations are taken from a group of writings called the Upanishads. Their compilation occurred more than three millenia ago, yet their feeling and content surprisingly orients the mind of the reader in the same direction as those descriptions from the Christian saints listed. One finds in these writings less of a purely rational glorification of God in which abstract or theological terms would be used. The formal, impassable distance between man and God is closed. There is diversity of description which does not stand in opposition to each other. Yet in the formal, exoteric teachings of the churches, one would not expect these descriptions; they are too optimistic. They belong to those who left the valley and climbed the mountain.

Orthodox Faith and Esoteric Realization

As we have seen, there are two orientations to religious consciousness. The esoteric mentality respects the conventional beliefs, dogmas, rites and other symbols so revered by the exoteric believer. He simply enriches himself beyond them. The typical exoteric believer, however, in his allegiance to his faith symbols, usually cannot accept any other interpretation.

This rigidity seems uncalled for in that neither rational philosophy nor faith beliefs can completely elucidate the divine reason. Our senses, nervous system, brain and discursive mind are primarily oriented to tangible realities and the relations among these realities. People find it more manageable to deal with the stuff and flux of everyday realities, such as working at a job and raising a family, than they do with pondering the subtle intricacies of God's presence in the human soul. While theologians and preachers may remind believers of these spiritual possibilities, the typical believer just does not feel that close to the reality mentioned even when he accepts them in faith. The biblical words are there to inspire and offer solace. But the typical believer, in exoteric faith, does not live from a personal consciousness that would confirm the above quotations.

In the esoteric experience, the participant instantly recognizes the impossibility of adequately transferring its meaning into clear, definite and familiar language. Something has happened to the person which cannot be located on the familiar horizon of everyday life and normal religious practices. No word or symbol can possibly be the only one that attempts to convey the reality. Just as the Eskimo has dozens of words to describe what those living in less wintry conditions would simply describe as "snow," so does the esoteric mind know the sense of joyous frustration in symbolizing the myriad experience of transcendence.

A tendency develops in the historical progress of a religious tradition, both individually and in community, that hardens its symbols which represent the divine or transcendental realm. The necessity for communication, for soliciting newcomers, for declaring publicly the unique opportunity presented by the believing church requires symbols that express the specific meaning of the church's existence. But as the followers organize and extend their influence to society, their religious symbols take on a rigidity that was unlikely at their inception. Now one is saved, redeemed, baptized, born again, only in *this* manner and only by *this* church affiliation. The exoteric symbols are so fixed that they have restricted the universality of divine truth and its validity to these definite and finite expressions.

The exoteric mentality attributes to a conditioned form – be it a scriptural emphasis, a ritual, a dogma or private sentiment – an absoluteness that only the formless and total truth possesses. Consequently these symbolic forms take on an implacable authority that negates the possibility for transcendence on any other terms. The religious conclusion amounts to this: it is our way or else eternal perdition.

The mistake is not new. Roman authorities after Caesar felt justified in persecuting the Christians for refusing due reverence to the Roman gods. While such religious harassment has diminished in the West, there always resides the possibility for the exoteric symbols to assume a self-sufficiency that will not tolerate exceptions or development.

No form can ever be adequate in conveying formless truth. To insist otherwise is to mistake a particular form for the substance. To describe an event of prodigious value even at a pedestrian level, in a multitude of words, always leaves room for more explanation. If divine truth is intelligible (and otherwise there could be no communication), it cannot be reduced to rational propositions alone. Thus, statements of beliefs may be true, but they cannot close out all other accounts.

The exoteric approach may threaten the possibility for a believer to develop beyond his conventional beliefs. A psychologist interested in religious phenomena, Abraham Maslow, once remarked that "what happens to many people . . . is that they simply concretize all of the symbols, all of the words, all of the statutes, all of the ceremonies, and by a process of functional autonomy make *them*, rather than the original revelation, into the sacred things and sacred activities. That is to say, this is simply a form of the idolatry (or fetishism) which has been the curse of every large religion."[17]

Maslow would not be alone in his criticism. A study of the history of the versions of Christianity would aptly confirm his observation. His telling point comes now: "In idolatry the essential original meaning gets so lost in concretizations that these finally become hostile to the original mystical experiences . . ."[18]

The exoteric believer, in allegiance to his beliefs, overlooks the historical origins of religious truth. An attitude of faith is primary until one reaches its clarifying ground; faith then becomes secondary and derivative once the transcendental experience has occurred. The origin of religious consciousness that gives a justification to faith is an unsurpassable experience. This revealing experience unintentionally shatters the conventional beliefs and the customary personal and mental limits implied by them. This revelation does not so much contradict as expand the believer's consciousness. The revelatory experience has such stupendous intelligibility about it that both the rational mode of consciousness and the faith mode are, to describe its reality, inadequate but helpful. Meeting the absolute defies articulation. What could Moses say about the burning bush and Mount Horeb? What could the disciples report about their pentecostal event? What can any man or woman utter after their encounter with absolute being?

People do not meet absolutes in the market place. Instead the realm of nature and culture is proliferated with specific and limited kinds of being. Our human minds find it comfortable and accessible to engage particular beings. There are no examples, no precedents, for meeting absolute being. Whatever one attempts to call the revelation, it still exceeds all rational categories. The esoteric, then, who is pursuing this orientation or has encountered the revelatory experience would approach his former beliefs with a recognition of their value but without entrapping himself in their parochial boundaries.

Having sensed or tasted the revelation, the esoteric person can no longer survive at the level that is comfortable for the exoteric community. Now he sees the essential relativity of institutional religions wherever they may prosper on this planet. He knows from hs own experience that divine truth takes on many guises necessarily for its communication in time and space. The ordinary intelligence does not deal with pure truth but truth in piecemeal fashion. He knows that conditioned truths imply their unconditional source. The direct revelatory experience of the divine reality has a depth and breath that simply cannot be interpreted from the confinements of mere exoteric beliefs.

By the nature of the experience, no revelation is total. Whether one speaks of Krishna, Moses, Buddha, Jesus, Mohammad or any sage or saint, what these personages reveal is restricted by their human form. The absolute as such cannot be experienced within finite realities. Divineness as expressed in a human individual, even when the followers identify him as God, is still not God pure and simple but an embodiment of divinity. In this way, revelation makes divinity available through a living medium which cannot help but limit the presentation. The rational mind which allows faith in the first place cannot assimilate a revelatory or transcendental experience. Even religious faith, admitting it as a kind of knowing, cannot assimilate the divine experience. The esoteric's experience is of such a universality that it cannot be focused adequately into the concepts and categories of beliefs or theological statements. These latter speculations about the divine reality cannot satisfy once an immediate and direct experience of unconditioned reality occurs.

Yet there remains for most people the assistance of beliefs and dogmas. The distractions and competitiveness of cultural existence make it difficult to search for the exoteric experience. Those searching for the meaning of life need reminders – beliefs, codes, rituals, scriptures, even taboos – to help sustain their motivation. For most the achievement requires a sense of communal support.

Consciousness and the Role of Transcendence
Spiritual growth is a maturing in the awareness of transcendental reality. Both the exoteric and the esoteric admit the necessity for symbols of transcendence. The ordinary believer acknowledges the existence of transcendental values by his act of faith. This act allows the exoteric believer to have a passive participation in the meaning of his beliefs. There may yet come moments of spiritual stress that test his faith conviction. The events of life will contend, at times, with his faith commitment. But the purpose of the symbols is to foster personal growth in the will to believe. The act of faith assumes a position of authority that permits the believer to connect everything else in the church. To avow, to testiify, to witness to the faith becomes

in the mind of the believer the symbolic goal of his church membership. For believers, faith is all.

The esoteric views the purpose of transcendent symbols as beckoning him beyond their inspiration. Beliefs and dogmas are the road maps that lead one on a voyage to an experiential goal. The goal is not to testify to orthodox faith, but to realize transcendence in one's lifetime. Consequently, the language of symbols must evoke one to pursue transcendence, not merely believe in it. If at all, belief becomes a tool for exploration and not a secure barrier of scriptural promises.

In yoga philosophy there is a recognition that everyone carries an unrestrictive desire to reach out to transcendence. This capacity for unconditional existence becomes articulated differently in religions and societies. Since the adult members of a church have all experienced, one way or another, the persistent urge within themselves to outgrow childish ideas, prejudices and misinformation, why curtail this fundamental drive at the borders of faith? When faith is put into the context of growth and consciousness, then there would seem to be room for development. Since we recognize stages of biological and emotional growth in everyone, could not the same conscious life force continue in its spiritual odyssey past the borders of faith?

In addition to that level of consciousness that exercises reason and faith, there is a richer more intuitive level. There, at that level, the remarks quoted earlier assume their justification. One's objection rises: How can the typical believer propose that he could attempt such a goal, even if the possibility would exist? It is a matter of priorities. If you want anything out of the ordinary, then you have to take the precautions. How important is this to you? Is there a career, a profession, a vocation whose requirements do not involve rearranging one's habits and preferences? To actualize transcendence could hardly cost less. Finally, the believer must decide for himself whether faith and beliefs are there to postpone transcendence or be a goad in realizing the possibility now.

CHAPTER 3

Yoga for Practical Christians

God said, "Let us make humans in our own image, in the likeness of ourselves, and let them be custodians of the fish of the sea, the birds of heaven, the cattle, all the wild beasts and all the reptiles that crawl upon the earth. So God created human beings in the image of God's self, in the image of God they were created, male and female God created them. . . . And God saw all God had made and indeed it was very good:" (Genesis 1 26–27, 31).

It is disconcerting to see how, in general, Christians treat themselves as God's image. In the midst of scientific and technological advancement they are often found wanting in the appreciation of themselves as bodily and spiritual beings. Most Christians tend to ignore the most elementary physiological laws as well as their connection to their spiritual development. Is there a way that preserves the scriptural endorsement of human nature so that Christians can systematically develop themselves in body, mind and spirit?

The science of yoga responds to this problem by affirming the divine judgment about human nature. As a most positive and comprehensive approach to health and spiritual well-being, yoga confirms the Christian's acceptance of human nature as a priceless gift to be preserved and developed. In yoga one learns to live with the seasons, facing life as a whole, developing one's humanity to its fullest potential. For a Christian, the techniques and philosophy of yoga can serve as an invitation to foster the biblical injunction to perfect oneself as God's image.

The science of yoga belongs to an ancient source of perennial wisdom. The school of yoga that embraces both the theoretical and experiential dimensions of human nature is called *raja* yoga, or "the royal path." It is the most comprehensive tradition, among the schools of yoga, for it treats questions regarding physical health, diet, exercise, the development of virtue, the regulation of breath, the ordering of emotions, concentration and the development of intuitive awareness. Unless otherwise noted, when we speak of yoga throughout these pages, we will be referring to the royal path.

As a science, yoga has become increasingly recognized in the Western world, but often Christians mistake it for an Eastern religion. Yoga and Christianity are like two streams flowing from the same fountain of perennial wisdom. Each has a different approach in assisting human development. Like Christianity, yoga is broader than any one culture. To speak of yoga as a wisdom means that it transcends cultural labels; that it shares with other wise traditions a timeless quality that makes it a continual resource for human enrichment.

Yoga, then, is not an Eastern import. It is not a religion, nor an ethnic custom. That its traditional ground for thousands of years has been the Himalayan mountain region was a geographical advantage to its founders and not a boundary to its universality. Yoga remains free of ethnic, religious, political or social influence. Christianity shares an Eastern origin with yoga and likewise transcends both geographical and cultural boundaries that initially supported it. Does one speak of the circulation of the blood or the law of gravity as being Eastern or Western? Much less should anyone subscribe to yoga or Christianity on the mistaken association that they are indigenous to the Eastern world.

As a non-cultural contribution to human development, yoga is applicable to any citizen of any country. It is concerned about the basics of human nature as such. Christianity likewise offers universal values that inspire humankind without jeopardizing the cultural preferences of believers. Both yoga and Christianity share a common appreciation of human nature and its destiny that has a timeless character enabling their common vision to be implemented throughout history. They can be considered two candles joined in illuminating man's ignorance with the one flame of knowledge.

The classic scripture that reveals the heart of *raja* yoga is called *The Yoga Sutras of Patanjali*. The word *sutra* means "thread" and refers to the 196 aphorisms that comprise the codification of the centuries-old wisdom. These aphorisms are like jewels threaded together to form a beautiful necklace of truth. The sutras were written in a language that makes statements about the spiritual development of human nature without relying upon cultural or religious symbols. These coherent affirmations analyse the various powers and faculties of human consciousness both in itself and as it relates to the body. In addition, Patanjali indicates the technical exercises that actually prove the theoretical proposition enumerated. By reading the text, one is given a tour through the human mind in its pursuit of spiritual excellence. By performing these sutras under the direction of a competent teacher, one has a step-by-step manual for achieving the goal of complete human integration.

To put Christian minds at ease, it is important to remember that yoga does not displace religion. Yoga can no more threaten genuine religious beliefs than can a basic course in biology. Yoga's interest lies in the study of human nature and its unfoldment from the primary perspective of consciousness. It investigates questions concerned with the range of the human mind, the interrelationship between mind and body, the normal attitudes one should have in order to cope with life calmly and intelligently. These and other similar questions are treated extensively by the philosophy and psychology of yoga.

For society, yoga poses a critique of culture. Whenever society becomes complacent or discouraged with its current level of civilization, yoga quietly insists upon a special feature of human nature. No matter how bogged down or overwhelmed we may become with our involvement with society, we possess, according to yoga philosophy, a transcendental nature. In spite of our needless worries and tribulations, yoga reminds us that we are more than our body, our mind, our career, our success or failure with life, for we possess a center of wisdom and strength within that makes our nature wider than history.

In yoga philosophy, a distinction is made between human nature and human culture. People cannot help but identify with their ethnic origins or national territory. As a result, they forget that these qualifications denote, like the chopsticks of China or the saris of India, only a cultural preference. Within a society, cultural protocol only expresses the imaginative art of human communication; it cannot disclose universal insight for human development. Cultural customs are only temporary; they cannot resolve the quest for human happiness. On the other hand, yoga, being outside cultural frameworks, addresses itself to the root problems of life and the means to human fulfillment.

We all live in culture and history. We grow accustomed to our habitudes and cannot easily avoid being provincial and sectarian in our desires. Yoga recognizes that beneath the multitude of desires within the human soul there lies a fundamental one that is rarely satisfied – a desire to know experientially the ultimate meaning of human existence and the nature of human happiness.

What human existence means to you may not be what it means to me. This is true as long as we are speaking from a relative perspective. But is there a broader perspective, one that satisfies everyone regardless of race, creed or locale?

If one speaks in ultimates, there cannot be a diversity of goals. There may be, however, a diversity of means to achieve that goal. If the case were otherwise, if your version of ultimate human existence were opposite of mine, yet equally true, then there would be two human natures. Your nature would be type A, while mine would be type Z. We could not speak of the human family as being one. To some extent, people already practice this shortcoming by focusing on those factors that make them different from others. Human nature, though, is not composed of those factors or items that make someone different from his neighbor. Race, color, creed, bank account, vacation home are all only accidents. They are not essential to appreciating the basic unity of the living organisms called human.

The differences in personality are obvious but still this amazing variety does not prevent thoughtful reflection from discerning a common nature shared by all. Appraised of cultural differentiations, people still uphold themselves as one human family, one kind of being. The paradox is that people's actions do not always substantiate this universal truth. Thus wars continue.

Yoga, in its study of human nature, outlines its remarks from a universal perspective. Yoga does not explain how to be a better carpenter or Icelander. Yoga goes deeper and explains how the carpenter's or the Icelander's same human nature can reach its inner potential as a human being.

The yoga investigations of human faculties contribute to the psychological and moral heritage found in moral philosophy. The Christian understanding of the moral and intellectual virtues (Latin *vir/virtus*, meaning "power") is complemented by the *Yoga Sutras's* analysis of these same innate powers.

These powers became, in the yoga analysis, foundational attitudes that are naturally fostered by those who are striving to live humane lives. Yoga encourages the development of these attitudes as ten commitments (called the *yamas* and *niyamas*) to support the individual's growth towards self-realization. The five *yamas* guide one's relationship with other beings. They are:

ahimsa – the art of non-violence in thought, word and deed
satya – the art of truthfulness towards oneself and others
asteya – the art of non-stealing
Brahmacharya – the art of sexual continence
aparigraha – the art of non-attachment

The five *niyamas* guide one's attitude toward his personal conduct. They are:

> *saucha* – the art of purity that leaves one's mind unfettered by prejudicial thoughts as well as the body hygienically clean
>
> *santosha* – the art of contentment under all circumstances
>
> *tapas* – the art of spiritual fervor
>
> *swadhyaya* – the art of self-discovery
>
> *Ishwara pranidhana* – the art of acknowledging the divinity within

These maturing attitudes comprise the ingredients that allow for an integration of character, which, in turn, disposes the aspirant for realizing self-realization. These guide the aspirant in the face of unruly impulses and negative evaluations. Unless one learns to foster positive attitudes in meeting life's challenges, then the natural powers of mental and physical energy may turn self-destructive. In examining these guidelines one can find only a healthy and sound regard for cultivating human potentials. The ancient science of yoga attempts to treat all the basic principles of human nature that stimulate that nature's optimal fulfillment.

Let us examine the overlooked aspect of human nature called breathing as an example. Yoga principles do not treat breathing from a static point of view. Understanding yoga is not like studying Grey's anatomy classic. The emphasis of yoga is on a dynamic appreciation of human nature. Right at the start, yoga parts company from various fields of study by insisting that it cannot be authentically understood except as a dynamic discipline. Yoga is yoga and understood as yoga only in the act of applying it. The meaning of yoga dawns in the act of performing it, not from reading about it.

Yoga's emphasis on breathing is a case in point. Human breath as a subject of study offers little stimulation for reflection by most people. Yet the rate, depth and rhythm of one's breath constantly influences the way one feels, the thoughts one thinks and the zest with which one faces life. Everyone breathes the same air with similar organs, but not everyone enjoys the maximal benefits from proper breathing. Yoga science recognizes that breathing is not a theoretical reflection but an activity that engages the entire person. Discovering that breath affects the whole nature of man, the founders of yoga probed the mystery of breathing by practicing different techniques for different effects upon human nature. They realized that specific exercises in breathing unify the mind and body into a healthier relationship. By practicing a simple form of diaphragmatic breathing one comes to know through that experience alone that a beneficial change has taken place in their overall feeling and thinking. One's concrete state of being can be altered, sometimes drastically. The act of proper breathing promotes a coordination between the body and mind that is obtainable by no other method. The end result is there because the laws of breathing, when properly stimulated, produce definite effects upon one's being. These effects can be verified under controlled experimentations. Thus the laws of breathing, discovered by yoga practitioners, are not the result of authoritative faith or persuasion; they remain the positive truths of using human nature according to its inherent laws.

From the continued practice of yogic breathing, one's self-understanding increases in and through the breathing practice that directly affects the expansion. A kind of inner learning takes place during the practice. An academic knowledge of the human respiratory system cannot change one's physical and spiritual condition. Yet knowing the respiratory system through the act of breathing – a different kind of knowing than abstract concepts – provides a self-knowledge that is unavailable to the book description of breathing.

Regulated breathing lays the foundation for self-understanding. One is not merely exchanging gases. The experiential performance of breathing improves the practitioner's sensitivity to his inner nature. One gains an awarenesss of controlling and studying his nature in a direct and immediate sense – a dynamic knowedge rather than a theoretical knowledge of one's being. Yoga establishes its rightful claim to true knowledge through practice, not through intellectual coherence. Verification is always made by the individual. One can immediately submit a particular practice to personal scrutiny. To embark on the practice of yoga is to enter, not an intellectual adventure, but a transformative process for which one accepts responsibility.

Obviously, yoga can be described with concepts. These reflected ideas of yoga are systematically and coherently outlined in two texts: *The Yoga Sutras of Patanjali*, as earlier discussed, and the *Samkhya Karika*. The concept of yoga, however, is not the revelation of its truth. Yoga's power comes not from the idea but from the actual evoking of the interior laws of man's nature. Like Christianity, which makes sense only when it is put into action, yoga postulates that people carry within themselves the impulse or appetite towards self-perfection. Men and women want to actualize their total nature, to experience life as richly, as enjoyably, as maturely as possible. The personal troubles they encounter, including emotional distress and disease, are symptomatic of their inability to regulate and develop this inherent appetite for life.

Yoga further recognizes that human nature is multileveled, a combination of vegetative, sentient, rational and intuitional forces that should function organistically for well-being. The inability, moreover, to achieve this integrated condition as an abiding state results primarily from ignorance. Yoga treats suffering as the temporary product of man's failure to understand himself, which can be eradicated through the discipline of true knowledge about his nature. All the dimensions of consciousness and all the levels of human nature must become involved in this holistic enterprise.

Yoga, therefore, is an applied philosophy of human nature.

This definition departs from the modern conception of philosophy as only a theoretically coherent version of life. Yoga's purpose is not to arrive at correct concepts in order to satisfy the intellect, but rather to stimulate the latent potentials in human beings that will bring them to final, conscious realization. With that aim in mind, it offers itself as a systematic program for peaceful living in full self-awareness. On that basis alone should yoga pass or fail.

Christians, in embarking upon the path of yoga, can only find therein a resource of knowledge that will provide an integration of body, mind and spirit for fulfilling the purpose of life.

CHAPTER 4

Yoga and the Sermon on the Mount

The Sermon on the Mount expresses the mind of Jesus more clearly than any other scriptural proclamation. It is a distillation of wisdom that summarizes Jesus' vision of the nature of human relationships and the attitudes of mind and heart for fulfilling human destiny. It is one of the most challenging programs for spiritual development elaborated in the history of spirituality. It is a public manifesto for Christian identity. In other words, it the criterion by which the world ought to judge the value of Christianity.

The written gospel words that have come down to believers fifty years after Jesus' Sermon have accumulated an expansion of meaning in the communities in which they were repeated. We are fortunate in having before us the final editing of those words. Although the Sermon was given in a Judaic–Roman culture, there are metaphors and symbols that ring out in the hearts of people a message of liberation and fulfillment.

The task of every generation is to examine this heritage using the tools of interpretation that can unlock the hidden depths contained therein. Every generation has the right to align the Sermon with the values and aspirations of its citizens. In this way the contrast and similarities provided by this confrontation of visions may challenge the examiner to see how the Sermon can contribute to life's meaning.

Every book needs an interpreter. The text of the Sermon is no exception in relying upon interpretive tools. Textual analysis relies upon many professional fields of knowledge in order to explicate the meaning. Philological studies, cultural archeology, even economics and sociological knowledge are used by exegetes and theologians for elucidating the significance of biblical passages. Everyone gains from this collaboration.

Theologians always borrow some principle of explication. After the Apostles, the Church Fathers used various rational disciplines such as Greek philosophy and psychology to elaborate the implications of the Gospels. Later Christian writers like Augustine used Platonic philosophy. In the high middle ages Saint Thomas Aquinas used Aristotle's works for elaborating biblical texts. Modern theologians like Bultmann, Tillich and Rahner show their reliance upon the philosophical thought of Martin Heidegger. In almost every instance it can be shown that biblical scholars and theologians utilized the sciences and knowledge at their disposal for opening the Bible wider to its readers. Any science or body of knowledge that shares a common subject matter with the Bible is a valuable aid as far as it goes with the investigation of biblical texts.

As a scientific tool for investigating human consciousness and for discerning various states of mind as evidenced in the Bible, yoga qualifies for this task. A Christian who studies and practices yoga will soon find that his efforts are complementary with many Christian insights that aid him in his pursuit of spiritual growth.

In this essay certain yoga terms and explanations will be offered to broaden the appreciation of biblical themes and passages. For revelation presupposes consciousness, whether in a Moses, an Esther, a Jesus or a Paul, and for the truths of the Bible to have a universal meaning, the understanding of revelation cannot be separated from man's self-understanding. Since human consciousness is the internal dimension of revelation, the Bible and yoga converge upon this same quest. While there are many valid approaches to studying the Sermon, such as from the standpoint of theology, morality, literary composition or historically, our concern will be an analysis of the Sermon from the standpoint of yoga psychology.

The Two Sermons

What we know today as the Sermon on the Mount is ascribed
to two writers, Matthew and Luke, in two separate books. The
more familiar version is found in Matthew's Gospel (Matthew
5:1 – 7:29) which is also the more descriptive. Luke's account
(Luke 6: 20–49) actually takes place on a plain after Jesus
descended the mountain. Matthew's broader version includes
many of Jesus' later teachings on Hebrew law which were given
to the crowds. This inclusion would be necessitated by the
fact that Matthew's audience was primarily Jewish. These later
passages are not included in Luke's version of the Sermon
because Luke wrote for the Gentile converts.

We should not be surprised by these and other omissions when
the Gospels are compared. Each Gospel after all was gathered
from and prepared for a distinctly different audience. Matthew's
concern was for Jewish converts to Christianity. His reliance
upon the Law, the Prophets and the writings (the threefold
division of the Jewish Bible) would necessarily be required for
his listeners to appreciate that Jesus is the Torah's fulfillment.
In Matthew's Gospel Jesus is the new lawgiver, fulfilling the
role of Moses as well as being the new David, the prince of the
new kingdom. Obviously Matthew will connect as much of the
Old Testament figures and passages to the career of Jesus as
possible.

Luke, on the other hand, would not be interested in the
Hebrew prefigurements since he could not presuppose familiarity with Jewish customs and practices in his audience, and
they might even have been a source of alienation at the time.
Modern Christians, however, cannot help but feel inspirational
power revealed by these passages.

The scene for the Sermon portrays Jesus distancing himself
from the crowds and teaching, not standing as was expected of a
Jewish teacher, but sitting as characteristic of the master/disciple
relationship. He spoke specifically to his disciples. "Seeing the
crowds, he went up the hill. There he sat down and was joined

by his disciples. Then he began to speak. This is what he taught them" (Matthew 5:1). Scriptural research indicates that the Sermon was meant exclusively for Jesus' disciples and not for the general public. Luke's account supports the theory that the Sermon was meant only for the disciples. According to Luke, the Sermon begins, "Then fixing his eyes on his disciples, Jesus said . . ." (Luke 6:20).

In the Sermon Jesus describes the nature of the perfect disciple. He attempts to convey the spirit of his New Law which should animate the aspirant. Later, as the scene was recounted in the Christian communities, the Christians were inspired by this portrait in hopes of being imbued with the same spirit. Consequently, the Sermon indicates much more than moral qualities assocated with a civil character. It indicates a total spiritual transformation.

The Beatitudes

Jesus' Sermon begins with his description of the beatitudes. He is actually relating Old Testament wisdom and placing it in a new context. If one were to read in the prophet Isiah, Chapter 1 and the Psalms 1:1, 32:1, and 41:2, one could get a sense of the continuity of insight that Jesus is conveying to his students.

Every beatitude starts with the word "blessed." Blessed indicates a condition of good fortune or good prospects. Since the kingdom will be everlasting, the notion of "blessed" includes more than a temporal condition. A blessing can be a temporary enjoyment, as often is the case in many passages of Torah or the Old Testament. There the follower of Yahweh may enjoy good health, prosperous economy, abundant crops and herds. Yet this good fortune is transitory. It's good while it lasts. In Jesus' words, however, the blessing conveys an everlasting element, for these are the qualifications for the reign of the kingdom of God.

Let us now take a brief look at the beatitudes. Although Luke's account lists only four beatitudes (and four curses), since these are also listed by Matthew we shall pursue Matthew's longer version, which is also more common to modern Christians.

First Beatitude: "Blessed are the poor in spirit for theirs is the kingdom of heaven." The poor in spirit indicates an interior purification of desires for sensible things. Objective wealth is of no concern. The phrase underscores an attitude of inner detachment from external possessions. One of the essential qualities recorded by the Yoga Sutras for achieving spiritual growth is an abiding sense of detachment from craving external things. This quality of the human spirit recognized by the Sutras is endorsed universally among spiritual teachers. The average mind becomes distracted by the array of attractions provided in one's culture. A certain inner distancing from these otherwise healthy ambitions for possessions needs to be acquired in order to sustain a spiritual perspective. Likewise a subtlety enters the aspirant's path as he strives to attain spiritual advancement. Here, too, one must have a higher degree of detachment from the tendency to flatter oneself in spiritual progress. Detachment produces a feeling for one's spiritual need. And so the poor in spirit will one day inhabit the kingdom.

Second Beatitude: "Blessed are the gentle, for they shall inherit the earth." This passage is a repetition of Psalm 37:11 where the meaning conveys a gentle or considerate disposition: "The humble shall have the land for their own to enjoy untroubled peace." In the biblical mind the land was a divine inheritance given by God to his faithful ones. Thus, to possess the land meant to possess God. Gentleness indicates an attitude of nonviolence, the *ahimsa* of the *Yoga Sutras.* Amidst the unexpected changes and pressures of life, there are many occasions for losing one's temper or becoming upset with life. Not only does this provoke violence upon one's nervous system, it creates a habit of mind that can destroy social relations. Gentleness is a sign of strength. It means one can cope with the vagaries of life with a gentle hand. Gentleness presumes great discipline and thus the gentle ones stand ready to receive their spiritual inheritance.

Third Beatitude: "Blessed are those who mourn, for they shall be comforted." People often mourn over a failure of a task or project that should have worked out. Jesus himself was no stranger to this kind of mourning: "My heart is nearly broken with sorrow" (Matthew 26:38). There are times when even the best of plans will not materialize, when even injustice, privation and death itself seems to snatch at our happiness. What this beatitude seems to be affirming is that even this sorrow shall also pass, and that an everlasting comfort awaits the soul.

Fourth Beatitude: "Blessed are those who hunger and thirst for righteousness, for they shall be satisfied." In the Old Testament one hungers and thirsts for the word of God. The personal possession of the word produces righteousness by placing the believer into the attitude for conducting himself according to the spirit of the word. The biblical notion of hunger and thirst would be an illustration of the fundamental appetite for truth which is the basis for yoga's quest as well. People in all walks of life ultimately want to know the truth; they are unsatisfied with anything less. Jesus is building upon this natural exegency by showing how those who sustain it, who are true to it, will one day be satisfied with nothing less than divine truth. The desire for righteousness places the disciple into the attitude for conducting himself according to the divine spirit within.

Fifth Beatitude: "Blessed are the merciful, for they shall obtain mercy." In the Old Testament it is written: "Shall a man refuse mercy to his fellows and yet seek pardon for his own sins?" (Sirach 28:4). To the Hebrew mind the theme of showing mercy is always a sign of God's mercy towards mankind. One shows mercy because one has experienced mercy. The concern and care for the welfare of others is precisely the foundation of *raja* yoga, for the very first quality of spirit that the *yamas* build upon is *ahimsa*, which means non-hurting, its positive side being compassion. Hence we find in Buddhist yoga that compassion is the highest virtue. Were not the Christians known by how much they loved one another? Empathy with the poor and the weak indicates a relationship between the doing of mercy and the receiving of mercy. This direct cause–effect relationship coresponds to the concept of *karma* in yoga and in the Gospels. Compassion at the human level reveals the highest form of love.

Sixth Beatitude: "Blessed are the pure in heart, for they shall see God." To the Jewish mind it was impossible to look upon God and live. Here Jesus shockingly reverses this belief and insists that seeing God is a possibility. One need only be pure in heart. Pure hearts have nothing whatsoever to do with purity from sin or even chastity. It is rather an integrity of outlook motivated by noble principles – the magnanimous person. The same individual is mentioned in the Torah as the "righteous" or the "just" one. These are the ones who respond fully to God's gift of life, for only these can express an unbounded generosity of spirit. This generosity of spirit prepares consciousness for experiencing higher realities. The same insight is proffered in Sutras 2:41 where from mental purity arises perfect self-knowledge.

Seventh Beatitude: "Blessed are the peacemakers, for they shall be called sons of God." Peace, according to Augustine, signifies the tranquility of order. Order is not a static term. To preserve the order of life requires a dynamic commitment calling upon all one's energies. Throughout the Gospels God is portrayed as a God of peace; Jesus himself is described as the prince of peace. The notion of sonship indicates a perfect communion with God. With that ordered relationship prevailing between God and man, one can be a doer of peace. The practice of yoga produces a new sense of order within, for yoga is the middle path between extremes. The integration of mind, body and spirit through spiritual practices recovers a sense of tranquility that can be borne to others. The whole effort of the Jewish notion "son of God" expressed a mission of restoration. The end result of that restoration is peace.

Eighth Beatitude: "Blessed are those who are persecuted for righteousness' sake, for theirs is the kingdom of heaven." Both Jesus and his followers encountered persecution. While they did not seek to alienate others, they managed to incur all forms of opposition to their projects. To live a lifestyle of integrity and honesty may not always be appreciated in every social environment. Only those striving to be poor in spirit are equipped to withstand persecution that may come from following one's conscience. And yet there is no other way but to follow the impulse of truth and continue to give compassion to others. These are the credentials of one who is eligible for the kingdom.

The New Law of Inner Transformation

The beatitudes are expressions of the inner transformation that must take root in order for one to enter the kingdom. These characteristics, which constitute the unfolding of the awakened personality are proof that one has entered into the kingdom. The values espoused by the beatitudes exceed society's standard for success. For all its worth, the external world cannot satisfy the disciple once his inner spirit aims at achieving perfection. For those who have yet to experience the full entry into the kingdom, the beatitudes offer an encouraging consolation amidst their human condition.

When the spirit of the kingdom animates the disciple, the characteristics of the beatitudes will be witnessed by other people. In this way the disciple becomes the "salt of the earth" and the "light of the world" (Matthew 5:13–16) as instructed by Jesus after he spoke the beatitudes in his Sermon.

Already the scriptures had recognized that salt prevented corruption in many perishable foods (Leviticus 2:13, Ezekiel 43:24). As a condiment it was irreplaceable (Job 6:6). The Book of Sirach even considers it one of the "elements necessary for man's life." (Sirach 30:26).

The passage applying "light" to the disciples is an Old Testament borrowing. Israel was the light to the nations (Isaiah 42:6); the servant of Yahweh was called the same (Isaiah 49:6). Jesus also applied it to himself (John 8:12) and extended it to his followers (John 12:35, Luke 2:32).

Thus the injunctions for being salt and light are not stressing the performance of missionary activity as much as keeping an integrity of spirit. One will be successful in the eyes of Jesus precisely because he remains faithful to his new uprightness. On this basis can he truly be an active force purifying and leading others to enlightenment.

The transformation of the disciples into their new uprightness actually crowns, completes and prolongs the norms of the Old Testament. Jesus takes the moral norms of the mosaic law and enlarges and extends them by insisting upon their interior character. People may follow sound moral laws by rote, without actually assimilating them into their own spirit. In verses 21–48 of the Sermon Jesus selects some moral prescriptions from the law and shows in six examples how these are now to be conducted by his transformed disciples. True morality emerges when the human spirit consciously accepts its own inherent ideals.

Under the Old Law one refrained from murder. Under Jesus' New Law there must be no anger, no insulting remark. One does not come to God without first reconciling himself to his fellow men. Instead of multiplying oaths to God, let us now have unfeigned sincerity with one another. While Jesus only enumerates a few concrete examples, the import of his meaning is obvious. Unless there is an elevation of one's ideal of perfection, these prescriptions cannot be fulfilled.

For example, the *ius talionis* (an eye for an eye) was inbred in the Middle East. It was considered an act of cowardice not to return vengeance for injustice committed against oneself. Jesus is not preventing one from resisting an unjust attack nor eliminating injustice to society; he refuses to condone someone's reacting out of vengeance or returning evil for evil. Retaliation must now give way to a higher justice.

The Impossible Goal: Perfect as the Father

In his Sermon Jesus brings love of neighbor to its summit: include your enemy. His phrase is a dramatic way of expressing a profound truth, i.e., love everyone. Here is the hallmark of Christianity. For someone to express universal love, to be what God is in his essence, makes one divine according to Jesus. One enters on equal footing with Jesus himself: "You will be sons of your Father in heaven" (Matthew 5:45). The goodness of universal love which includes even enemies now presents human beings as the fulfilled image of the heavenly Father.

Finally, Jesus announces the paradoxically impossible: be perfect as your Father is perfect (Matthew 5:48). The standard of achievement, the criterion of performance, is nothing less than infinite divine perfection. Human ingenuity, high moral standards, Nobel peace prizes, all fade into insignificance upon this outrageous demand. No less is expected of the disciples than a transcendental conduct.

All the beatitudinal qualities could be reasonably appreciated as ideals to strive towards and eventually achieve. The final instruction, however, to become perfect seems beyond human capability. Jesus seemingly demands an impossible quest. Christian morality is rigorous enough, but to require a transcendental elevation!

Perhaps Jesus' assertion should be taken as a simile? The context of the Sermon will now allow for this diminishing interpretation. A sense of the impossible conclusion fits the pattern of Jesus' thoughts. As unpredictable as his statements may be, they are nonetheless not entirely inconsistent with his earlier demands.

For many church-affiliated Christians, the Sermon on the Mount stands upon an untouchable pedestal of human conduct, an inspiring motif but hardly achievable. The paradox remains: how can frail human beings in their wildest imaginings compare their potential with the infinite resources of the creator?

The Kingdom Hidden in Parables

In helping to resolve this incredible impasse, let us recall some important clues throughout the New Testament. One discovers, first of all, in reading all the Gospels, that Jesus preferred to explain his message only to the disciples. The same message was offered to the public in cryptic parables. To understand parables is like solving riddles: one needs the key. But the key was never handed to the public. This omission does not receive the significance today that it possessed in his time.

Every Christian and biblical scholar recognizes the importance of Jesus' message for the world. Whether one describes the message as salvation, redemption, liberation, glorification or resurrection, they are simply partial attempts to reveal the basic overall proclamation: the kingdom of God is at hand.

Keeping this unparalleled good news in mind, one still finds that the kingdom is never explained. Its significance remains a secret, couched in enigmatic phrases that elude the general public. This is not a private evaluation but precisely the judgement the Gospels narrate about the matter.

> When he was alone, the twelve, together with the others
> who formed his company, asked what the parables meant.
> He told them, "the secret of the kingdom of God is given
> to you, but to those who are outside everything comes in
> parables" (Mark 4:10–11).

A careful examination of the Gospel parables shows that out of

the sixty-three parables of Jesus, forty-one parables are explained
– twenty-eight to the disciples, but only thirteen to the crowds.
At the same time twenty-two are not explained at all - seven
left unexplained for the disciples, but fifteen left unexplained
for the crowd. Those parables concerned with the kingdom are
never explained to the crowd.

Matthew records a conversation that the disciples had with
Jesus about his reluctance to explain the kingdom to the interested crowd:

> Then the disciples went up to him and asked, "Why do you
> talk to them in parables?" "Because," he replied, "the
> mysteries of the kingdom of heaven are revealed to you, but
> they are not revealed to them" (Matthew 13:10–11).

The use of the word "mystery" here is identical in the text with
the word "secret" used above in the quotation from Mark.
The meaning of mystery refers to the divine transcendental
knowledge of the kingdom. It does not mean that the kingdom
is unintelligible, but that its significance exceeds rational
analysis. Mystery thus indicates such richness of truth that the
rational mode of understanding cannot grasp it.

Is the Kingdom Closed to Ordinary Christians?

The question comes to this: if neither the crowds understood
nor the Gospels exposed the kingdom, where does that leave
Christians? To say that Jesus himself is the secret does not really
answer the question. Jesus quite obviously taught certain truths
which affected his disciples in a radical manner. Not everyone
who believed in Jesus could perform as the disciples. To know
the mystery was to possess the key to the kingdom; this knowledge could not be information, but only experiential.

Jesus knew the mystery and could lead others into the
kingdom. The mystery-knowledge could not be conveyed in
ordinary expressions, since people had no experience of the

kingdom. Parables could help because of their symbolic characteristics. There is more knowledge in a parable than the surface
meaning exposes. The words of a parable have some relationship to the common experience but simultaneously the full
meaning passes beyond the ordinary, rational interpretation.
The words may appear so enigmatic that the mind cannot
fathom any meaning, or the interpretative possibilities are apparently so broad that a definite assurance of meaning eludes the
mind.

Being an Eastern teacher, Jesus teaches not for the sake of
intellectual satisfaction, but to engage the whole person of the
student. Reading the Gospels is not a very intellectually exciting
task. No doubt the passages reflect Jesus as quite intelligent, but
his efforts in teaching were not to convey ideas alone, but the
deepest truths of life: What is the purpose of existence? What is
man's real destiny? How does one attain it? What is the true
nature of God? These were the kinds of questions that he
provoked in his audiences.

To assimilate Jesus' teachings was to accept a change in one's
life. Growth-oriented, personalistic development, healthy self-
image – all these terms of human psychology – could apply to
his method. These applications are insufficient, however,
without the prior understanding of the mystery of the kingdom.

Jesus remarks that he who has ears to hear will hear. The
truths of the Sermon will be intelligible only to those who have
the capacity to understand. His remark points up the relationship
between the knower and the ability to discern the reality
represented in symbolic form. The kingdom is preeminently an
inner reality not readily perceptible by men. The ability to
discern the kingdom's meaning has a direct bearing upon the
disposition of the human spirit.

Knowledge is always a function of the being of the knower.
To alter the capacity to know, the very nature of the knower
must change. Presenting new items for knowing does not affect
the inner capacity of the nature. Man's natural everyday mode

of knowing is discursive. As long as man identifies with his discursive manner of knowing, as long as he thinks that thinking is the highest activity for grasping reality, then the kingdom remains closed to him. Even faith in the kingdom does not gain much for the believer. Human belief in the kingdom merely alleges that the kingdom exists, but it does not disclose its secrets. Reason, like belief, finds only circumstantial clues. Neither is able to resolve the mystery.

To return to the conduct of those who can manifest the beatitudes, there is a relationship between their inner state and the outer activity in human action. To demonstrate the behavior of the Sermon in their daily lives, the disciples require an interior state of mind and heart that improves but does not nullify the normal virtues of good citizenship. As mentioned, the actions of any nature flow from the being of that nature. In order for the disciples to live the Sermon their inner nature had to change. Whether one calls it growth, evolution, expansion, the inner dynamics of knowing and loving had to undergo a drastic increase. This inner change cannot be equated with an intellectual broadening of the mind. The secret of the kingdom is not a bright new idea. To acquire new ideas about the world or self or even God cannot account for the behavior recognized in one possessing the beatitudes, understanding the parables, being a son of the Father, performing wonders and reaching perfection.

In describing the kingdom, Jesus is not talking about an idyllic territory. The kingdom is his symbolic expression for an inner transformation of spirit – what the Gospels call the "new man," the reborn event. To transform the nature of man is to bring the potentials of man's mind and heart, his cognitive and affective dimensions, into a superior actuality. The being of man changes. An interior change of this magnitude is associated with an intensification of the life principle within him. Life's power must increase.

The Kingdom As The Awakened Life Force

In yoga, the individual life force is known as *devatma shakti*. The kind of change demanded for the perfect disciple's performance is truly accomplishable provided the *shakti*, or life force within, manifests a higher integration. As the life force intensifies, so the cognitive and affective aspects of one's nature change accordingly. With the life force stimulated into new abundance, it directly increases one's ability to know and love. Even more than a myopic person beginning to have normal vision, or someone with lifelong color blindness suddenly perceiving colored objects, the conscious powers of one's being are so enormously amplified that the former capacities appear as a lesser nature. Scripture refers to this as "the old Adam."

Spiritual development as known in ancient scriptures has a definite order to it. The expansion of the life force does not happen mechanically or in a haphazard manner. A disciple undergoes a long preparation, for the amplified energy of life must find the properly tilled soil in which to grow. Since human nature utilizes a body, the necessary physical preparations are indispensable. Mind and body cooperate in this transmutation. A maturer integration of the life force eventually expands the field of consciousness to include intuition, a way of knowing that does not require concepts, but puts one into direct contact with any knowable object.

With the intensification of the life force, latent powers of human nature reveal themselves, thus challenging man's previous assumptions about self-limitations. Jesus remarked that he came to give life in abundance. Life is something to experience. And certainly the Gospel accounts show that the disciples are being led through life experiences that finally alter their self-understanding.

The increase in the life force, controlled and directed, leads to wisdom, an understanding of "heaven and earth." This phenomenon is reflected in the water initiation of Jesus. Here the ascetic John leads Jesus through a consciousness-raising event. The passages about the heavens opening and the dove of peace descending are insertions from the Genesis account of creation which describe the power of consciousness to manifest its creativity as the cosmos. As applied to the initiation story, the same creative life force transfuses through Jesus, producing a cosmic awareness. Jesus understands his nature and the range of his powers through this experience. Since Jesus is now the Father's son, he has entered into the kingdom.

From this juncture in his life, Jesus preaches and prepares his disciples for the same experience. They too are called to be sons of the same Father, to realize their divine nature in conscious fashion. The inner transformation achieved by the intensification of the divine life force can now account for the superior morality of the disciples. Their whole attitude towards life and death, material possessions, ranking of prestige, endurance of pain and obstacles, ability to relate to others, all these aspects of the human personality are radically improved with the self-knowledge provided by the expansive life force. They have found the key to the kingdom: the awakening within of the divine life that stirs them to live a transcendental life of God-like awareness.

One can now understand that the experience of this transformation could hardly be put in words, let alone parables. As far as revealing the exact techniques of the initiations, they were always sheltered from the crowd. Thus the Gospels speak of the good news of the kingdom but the keys are only given from teacher to disciple in readiness. Those preoccupied only with this world will never know that the mysterious knowledge of the kingdom is the self-transformation from the old Adam to the new, being born again into the spirit, that gives the ears to hear and the eyes to see the meaning of the parables and enables one to live the Sermon on the Mount.

CHAPTER 5

Yoga and The Jesus Prayer

One day in the middle of the nineteenth century, a young man attended religious services in a Russian Orthodox church. During the liturgy he heard the reading of Paul's letter to the Thessalonians. One text in particular struck his heart: "Pray without ceasing." His mind turned it over and over. Upon leaving the church he searched in his Bible to confirm what he had heard. He felt perplexed: How can one pray unceasingly? His urgency to satisfy this mandate forced him to search throughout the city for someone to explain the solution. Unsuccessful there, he wandered from city to village, village to monastery, monastery to city, always asking, always searching. Late one night he arrived at a monastery, having walked more than one hundred miles. He was welcomed in as a pilgrim. Immediately he implored anyone to explain the words of St Paul, as he had done hundreds of times before. An old *startsi* (spiritual master) was called. Upon hearing of our pilgrim's plight, the old man crossed himself and smiled, "Thank God, my dear brother, for having revealed to you this unappeasable desire for unceasing interior prayer." Then he taught the pilgrim the centuries-old method known as The Jesus Prayer. The pilgrim searched no longer, but spent the rest of his life praying without ceasing.[1]

The story of the pilgrim highlights an ancient practice indigenous to Eastern Christianity. The methodical use of this prayer practice has been described from the Russian version of the *Philokalia*, a compendium of teachings and diaries from the Desert Fathers, the Greek Fathers and theologians of Byzantine spirituality, from St Anthony in the third century up to modern times. In these writings, a unique form of meditative prayer is explained. It has been customarily practiced by monks of Eastern Christianity throughout the centuries. St Benedict of Nursia, the founder of Western monasticism, did not include this prayer method in his Rule for monastic life, and thus it has not been known in the spiritual traditions of the West.[2] Only in the twentieth century has it been rediscovered for contemporary Western spirituality.

The method, known as The Jesus Prayer, consists of the simple, unvariable formula: "Lord Jesus Christ, Son of God, have mercy upon me"[3] repeated again and again. Ideally, in learning the prayer, the aspirant approaches a *geront* or *staretz* (titles for a spiritual advisor) for the proper instructions. The inspiration for the formula is grounded in the Bible and the meditations of the Greek Fathers. In 1351 an orthodox council officially approved the doctrinal justification for the prayer. This ecclesiastical achievement was largely due to the defending efforts of a fourteenth-century monk, Gregory Palamas of Athos, who later died as the Archbishop of Thessalonica in 1359. The written material required for the practice of the prayer was included in the *Philokalia*, "the love of spiritual beauty", composed in the eighteenth century.

The purpose of The Jesus Prayer is not merely ritualistic or devotional. Prayer had always been appreciated by the Christian East as the primary means for growth in self-knowledge. In The Jesus Prayer also an interior transformation is sought that leads to what the Greek Fathers called *theosis*, or the spiritualiz-ation of the personality.

Hesychasm, a spiritual tradition that dates back to the third century, uses the Jesus formula as one of its forms of inner prayer. The Hesychast monks (Hesychast means "the tranquil one") were especially noted for using this meditation as the chief means for their spiritual development. They combined prayer

and meditation with breathing techniques as instructed by the
monk Nicephorus the solitary:

> You know. brother, how we breathe: we breathe the air in
> and out. On this is based the life of the body and on this
> depends its warmth. So sitting down in your cell, collect
> your mind, lead it into the path of the breath along which
> the air enters in, constrain it to enter the heart together with
> the inhaled air, and keep it there. Keep it there, but do not
> leave it silent and idle; instead, give it the following prayer:
> "Lord Jesus Christ, Son of God, have mercy upon me."
> Let this be its constant occupation, never to be
> abandoned. . . . These are the words of this blessed Father,
> uttered for the purpose of teaching the mind, under the
> influence of this natural method, to abandon its usual
> circling, captivity and dissipation and to return the attention
> to itself, and through such attention to reunite with itself,
> and in this way to become one with prayer and, together
> with prayer, to decend into the heart and to remain there
> forever.[4]

For a Christian practicing yoga this description is not merely
similar to, but the same as, *japa* yoga. The constant remem-
brance of a sacred sound, *mantram*, is commonly refered to as
japa. In yoga there is an ancient science of sound that permits
the aspirant to use a series of syllables for the precise purpose
of effecting an internal change in his consciousness. The inherent
power of the sacred sound, however, is not released in a mech-
anical way merely by its repetition. Preparation of the student,
proper intonation of the sound, and the guidance of a qualified
spiritual master make the practice effective. The function of the
geront/staretz served in the same capacity for the Hesychasts as
does a master teacher in the yoga tradition — as the germinator
of the seed–sound.

There is a certain naivete in the Western attitude that believes one can choose an appropriate *mantram* for oneself. This thinking finds its logical extension in the idea that the laws of *japa* are a matter of taste or fashion. If one is not satisfied with a particular *mantram*, why not select another? To their eventual discouragement such students will find that unless the laws of sacred sound are respected, their effects remain dormant.

The Hesychast method involved the combination of breathing and mental concentration at a definite area of the body. The combination of these two factors immediately identifies the process as being similar to ancient yoga. The Hesychast practice of converging breath, concentration and silent intonation at the heart region is a recognized yogic form of meditation. We have here an historical event in spirituality which links these two traditions. Whether these monks were informed yogis is not the issue. The descriptive facts of their method involve the laws of yoga whether the monks were cognizant of the tradition or not. Just how far back the monks started their method of prayer in this manner is difficult to trace, but the psycho-physical emphasis which facilitates the invocation of the name of Jesus corresponds to particular aspects of yoga and allows the ancient science to shed light upon this Christian method of prayer.

Yoga contributes to a greater understanding of this methodical prayer from its own laws of concentration. In the human body are definite gland and nerve centres, which, when interiorly focused upon by the mind, bring into play more subtle alterations of energy. The stimulation of a particular area through breathing and concentration affects a gradual expansion of those positive qualities associated with the spiritual development of that area.

For example, in the yoga schema of spiritual development, when the heart region is properly stimulated, an increase in the aspirant's ability to love is awakened. One becomes more sensitive affectively, especially to concerns of other people. A change of heart, a conversion, takes place. This change now influences one's vision of reality. One reverses selfishness. The

personality unfolds with compassion, leading one into a new
level of emotional integration.

In yoga terminology, the stimulation of this heart center, of
anahad chakra, purifies egocentrism. The same result is declared
by the Hesychast monks when they speak of the purified heart
being the abode of God. The method involves what the Fathers
call a "natural" process. It is a retraction from the excitement
of the senses, a silent intonation in rhythm with breathing and
an absorption of concentration upon the heart. Starting from
the human situation of "fallen nature", as described by the
monks, this technique attempts a return or restoration of one's
nature to its original pure state. Often accompanied by a feeling
of warmth around the physical heart, the technique gradually
leads to an awareness of one's higher self.

The Goal of the Hesychast: Theosis

The ultimate goal of the Hesychast method is the participation
in divine conciousness. A process of conversion is undertaken
in which attention is reversed from the external, created reality
towards the inner spirit. In this way a return or ascent inwards
to a divine status or *theosis* takes place. The method has similarities with Patanjali's classical yoga system. The *Yoga Sutras*,
like the Hesychast writings, designate a bodily and mental
regime that gradually disposes one to greater self-knowledge.
The coordinated disciplines bring a sense of mastery over human
nature, spontaneously including a calmness of spirit that spreads
throughout the body-mind complex. Amid that profound
peace, the Hesychast and the yogi intuit their real nature.

As a result of poor living habits, man's constitution is weak-
ened, his emotions embarrass him and his thinking is disori-
ented. Prone to grandiose illusions and selfishness, man's
inflated ego obscures his real nature. Hesychasm purposes an
organismic connection between body, mind and spirit. By
employing a psychosomatic method including posture,
breathing, attitude, and concentration, man's nature is

rehabilitated into full spiritual actuality. For this conversion to *theosis*, the aspirant must struggle with two stages of inner development called *praxis* and *theoria*.

Praxis

For the Hesychast *praxis* is similar to the moral code of yoga, the *yamas* and *niyamas*. The comparable asceticism aims at rectifying the dissipation of the senses and egotistical tendencies. Daily practice in bringing the senses and imagination under more rational direction permits less and less superfluous images and thoughts to distract concentration. In this way *enkrateia*, mastery of self, emerges. The Hesychasts insist that the experience of divine existence remains outside of man as long as he is unable to deal effectively with his thoughts and passions. Patanjali likewise remarks that unless one controls the fluctuations of the body-mind complex, his essential nature remains obscured: "Yoga is the control of the modifications of the mind. Then the seer is established in his own essential and fundamental nature."[5]

Theoria

The second phase of inner development results from the virtuous efforts of *praxis*. The purifying struggle to reorder the bodily and mental faculties throws more light upon the nature of the world. The inner rectifying of the appetites, along with the restraint of egotism, effects a cleansing, as it were, that allows one to be more objective. Reality is no longer a matter of personal preferences. The tempering of the senses produces a correcting effect upon the mental faculties. Self-deception about practical living wanes. One contemplates (*theoria*) the entire cosmos without imputing personal designs. Balance returns. The created world is seen with its relative merits. The purgative virtues, like yoga practices, effect discrimination. The Hesychast lives with what the yogi calls "meditation in action" – being in the world but not deceived about its nature.

According to St Maximus, *praxis* purifies the intellect and body. The reintegration of the intellect and emotions leaves the power of intelligence open. No longer dominated by the descent towards the material world, one's cleared intelligence now discerns the "divine wisdom invisibly contained in creatures."[6] Purgation has increased sensitivity, enabling one to recover the higher intuitive approach to reality. Instead of relying upon the limited framework of his rational faculty, he knows the world in a superior way – from within.

Passing beyond the superficial knowledge of created things, one apprehends their eternal essences. With an immense expansion of discernment, states Philotheus of Sinai, "this purified heart becomes an interior sky with its own sun, moon and stars, and circumscribes God, the Uncircumscribable, by the secret ascent of his vision."[7] Simultaneously with his illumination, according to St Macarius, the heart consciousness enlarges into a cosmic love: "the heart is aflame with love for every creature."[8] Saint Clement calls it *apatheia*, the cathartic control of the emotions that enables love to be strong and consistent.

Both Hesychasm and yoga describe an applied psychology for transforming human nature into its full actuality. The validity of either tradition lies not in authoritative declarations, however, but in the personal trial of the methods. In the daily testing through self-practice, the student can verify their intrinsic worth. Both traditions also respect the various levels of the body-mind complex. While the terminology can often be interchanged in either methodology, the Hesychast descriptions retain a religious symbolism and are less detailed in their presentation of the psychological stages than those of the *Yoga Sutras*. The traditions agree from the start that the student's emphasis is on "enstasy," a re-entering into oneself, as opposed to "ecstasy", the energetic moving outward from oneself to things. Both understand that the preliminary ascetical practices lead to the interiorization of the mind, culminating in an expansion of consciousness.

Both traditions respect the fundamental life principle as it functions in the entire body-mind complex. Since breathing and the heart's action are indispensable for life, both methods incorporate these facts of animation. The intrinsic relationship between these two vital functions, however, is the basis for more than a matter of ordinary physiology. While breath gives life to the body, the Hesychast considers the body as "the temple of the spirit."[9] He accepts a dependence between breathing and the infusion of the life spirit or *pneuma*; air serves as a vehicle for vitality to enter into man. From the spiritual point of view, the Hesychast sees *pneuma*, or the divine life breath, entering into man and making him into a holy temple. Already manifesting God's image, one becomes and continues to be enlivened with God's life force through the action of breathing.

The physiological connection between breathing and heart action for physical well-being corresponds to a higher level of psychological and spiritual integration. The rhythm of breathing indicates the condition of one's health as well as his spiritual vitality. The same life force, known as *prana* in yoga, promotes physical health as well as spiritual development. The Hesychast, like the yogi, recognizes the reciprocal communion between proper breathing and the lucidity of consciousness. According to St Nicephorus the Solitary:

> You know that our breathing is the inhaling and exhaling of air. The organ which serves for this is the lungs which lie around the heart, so that the air passing through them thereby envelops the heart. . . . Having collected your mind within you, lead it into the channel of breathing through which air reaches the heart, and together with this inhaled air, force your mind to descend into the heart and to remain there . . . the mind when it unites with the heart is filled with unspeakable joy and delight.[10]

The union of mind and heart in Hesychasm unexpectedly

concurs with the meaning of yoga – the science of the unification of man's powers for his full realization. The heart region is only one of several areas available to express various dimensions of man's personality. Although not described in the literature of the Hesychasts, these other centers of concentration which are associated with definite nerve ganglia throughout the body are fully elaborated in the yoga scriptures. Each of these seven major centers, called *chakras*, are responsible for characteristic personality development. The unfoldment of personality or spiritual restoration proceeds in either tradition from bodily diciplines and social virtues to inward concentration.

The early Christian communities symbolized their various practices in religious language which relied upon a close resemblance to biblical terms. Although the Gospels were their constant resource for clarifying their aim, still the natural explanation of becoming Christlike, the spiritual ascent, or *theosis*, can be equivalently interpreted from the holistic understanding provided by the yoga tradition. Both traditions assert the fundamental soundness of human nature. St Simeon remarked that human deification is not a supernatural addition to mundane nature; *theosis* does not make one into a two-tiered being of nature plus supernature. Rather, the monk continues, beneath ego and emotional cravings, which injure and blind one, lies a pure nature which "subsists fully, just as it was created."[11]

The Hesychasts do not speak of attaining something new but of recovering an inheritance already intrinsically possessed: the kingdom of heaven which lies within us. In order to discover this hidden kingdom, one must enter within and establish an interiorization of consciousness which is referred to as an "unknowing" or *agnosia*. Unknowing does not imply a condition of ignorance, but rather an unblemished awareness of reality without vested interests. One must leave behind his preference for the rational mode of uniting with the objects of his knowledge. One must actively seek an inward retraction from egotistical conceptualizations. The ego's liking for conceptualizing reality, even God, forms the last temptation. From the pervasive tendency, the ego must be purified. As one interiorizes, the effort to objectify what the mind most wants to idealize, namely God, must also be abandoned.

The divine essence is not an idea. Neither is the experience of divine life. Unlike the cosmos, God's intelligibleness can never qualify as an object of rational knowledge.

> The prayer of the heart must sweep away all imagination, both proper and improper . . . as wax melts in the fire, so does imagination disperse and disappear under the action of pure prayer through simple, imageless cleaving of the mind to God . . . since every thought enters the heart through imaging something sensory . . . so the light of the deity begins to illumine the mind when it is freed of everything and totally empty of form . . . as the Lord dwells not in temples built by human hands, neither does he dwell in any imaginings or mental concepts.[12]

Often Christians consider prayer and meditation as involving mental content. To elicit devotion, one must necessarily image the object of devotion. In the Hesychast tradition, however, the effort is to eliminate any fluctuation of the mind. Ordinarily the mind focuses its attention in a limited way upon the object of devotion. The Hesychast instead desires to eliminate the focus of the mind, allowing for an openness so that the light of divine consciousness may fill the heart.

In the late Middle Ages, books on Christian enlightenment reiterated this same approach to spiritual development. One finds in *The Book of Privy Counseling* such passages as:

> Reject all thoughts . . . see that nothing remains in your conscious mind save a naked intent stretching out toward God . . . leave your thought quite naked, your affection uninvolved and your self simply as you are. . . . [13]

The Flemish monk, Jan van Ruysbroeck, in his *The Adornment of the Spiritual Marriage* remarked that:

> enlightened men are, with a free spirit, lifted above reason into a bare and imageless vision wherein lies the eternal indrawing summons of the divine unity; and with an imageless and bare understanding they reach the summit of their spirits.[14]

John of the Cross states that: "the soul must be emptied of all these imagined forms, figures and images, and it must remain in darkness in respect to these internal senses if it is to attain divine union.[15]

The student on the path must be alerted, therefore, to conceptual straps, less he misidentify the level of ideas about God with the experiential intuitive knowledge of God. In their writings, the monks Callistus and Ignatius note:

> Since every thought enters the heart through imagining something sensory, so the light of the Deity begins to illuminate the mind when it is freed of everything and totally empty of form. . . .[16]

In its supreme conclusion the Hesychast path becomes strikingly similar to yoga. The positive unknowing or naked intellect is achieved through a process of stilling the mind. Dissociated from the slightest mental activity, subconscious or conscious, one breathes in undisturbed equanimity. An inner pacification that exceeds all descriptions reigns. In the undisturbed being of pure awareness without an object, the Hesychast and the yogi realizes his absolute nature. Reversing the externalization of consciousness, the vision of God becomes one with the vision of self. In perfect stillness, according to Evagrius, one has recovered his original state.

CHAPTER 6

Meditation: an Inner Science

Modern science is predicated upon its ability to verify its hypotheses. Verification is very important because it allows the investigator to objectify his thoughts. Astronomers, for example, may not be sensibly aware that there is another planet in space, yet they hypothesize its existence on the data of the movements of the other heavenly bodies. Through their ingenuity, scientific investigators can occasionally predict the discovery of a new body.

An elementary textbook in chemistry may assert that water, H_2O, boils at 212°F at sea level. If someone had never ascertained that fact in his own experience, he would have to assume that the statement was true. Various textbooks would repeat that ordinary water reaches a boiling point when heat is applied to the intensity of 212°F. But how does anyone really know that the statement is true? How does one know it makes sense? Is the text correct? Does water boil only at this specific point? The textbook author may be a close friend, or he may even possess a Nobel Prize, but are his assurances sufficient to make me feel secure in the knowledge that water boils at 212°F? Hardly. I want to know by experiencing the fact; otherwise doubts arise.

My mind is not satisfied with anything less than experience. In other words, a scientific demonstration requires first-hand knowledge. Second-hand knowledge, textbook statements, words from an authority cannot guarantee the security of knowledge.

Whether we are professionals who are striving to examine, or comprehend a section of reality, or just someone who is interested in life in general, we prefer real facts to wishful hoping. To stay close to the facts of life helps us to deal with the task of life. With facts, we have more possibilities for success in living than just hoping or praying that things will work out.

Nature is extravagant with her facts. So polymorphic is she in the display of her wares, that different intelligible approaches are possible to obtain factual knowledge. Man can be studied chemically, biologically, sociologically, psychologically, religiously, to name but a few. Each approach presupposes experiencing the facts, but seeks more than their enumeration. Cataloging facts is not science. How and why facts are facts is what forges scientific knowledge about our universe, and about ourselves.

People still refer to the universe as the cosmos. The word is borrowed from ancient Greek philosophers, the first scientists of the West, and means "order". The implication is that man, as well as any portion of nature, is a coherent reality wherein facts are related to facts constituting a unified totality. The cosmos is an inter-related reality, accessible to human intelligence which itself seeks to grasp its manifold order amidst the flux of life. The sciences, then, articulate the various connective orders lodged in the universe.

Man as the subject of scientific investigation offers a twofold approach for study. He can be investigated by many of the mathematical-empirical based sciences, like chemistry and physics, or he can be studied by the social-biological sciences like anthropology and psychology. But as a living, self-conscious being which internalizes the facts of the cosmos, man's investigation of himself is unique.

Man's interior world of consciousness is the field of scientific study called meditation. Meditation is the repeatable experiment in which man is both the investigator and his own laboratory. Man the investigator, in the practice of meditation, experiments directly with the source of experience – his own inner consciousness.

It may seem strange to investigate meditation in the West as a science when for centuries Christian monasteries and theological schools have espoused methods of meditation as an essential part of their religious practices. Until the recent interest by scientists in the nature and range of altered states of consciousness, prompted in part by biofeedback and mood-altering drugs, meditation has been associated with prayerful feelings and devotional attitudes. Yet today, the yoga science of meditation is recognized in research circles as an important subject matter with humanistic value. Focusing upon the natural phenomena involved in meditation and leaving aside the religious associations, scientists are able to perform legitimate investigations. Consequently, the various religious methods of meditation can benefit from the serious research being conducted upon man the meditator.

In its search for secure knowledge, science attempts to establish its hypothesis by eliminating the variables and finding the constant factors in an experiment. Likewise, meditation follows a similar procedure. As a science, meditation hypothesizes that the investigator can discover, in an orderly and repeatable way, universal knowledge regarding the nature of human consciousness. Moreover, the methodological procedure – the meditational process - is capable of verification. The investigator or practitioner can reproduce, by following the same procedure, sufficiently similar effects so that agreement on the results is confirmed. By submitting to principles of verification and predictability, meditation removes itself from the onus of a strictly private experience and allows for objective scrutiny.

From our presentation, meditation may be classified more as an applied than as a theoretical science. The investigator/ practitioner of meditation is not studying his thought patterns and operations of mind just to know that they exist, but to obtain definite results from this investigation. Studying the mind is not on a par with studying the subject matter of physics, chemistry or astronomy. The mind in itself is on a different plane of reality than the atomic structures of matter.

Another comparison may aid here. When one turns from physics to biology, one is confronted with a higher plane of reality. Biology, being the study of living organisms, is obviously a different field from theoretical physics. Since there is a radical difference in the subject matter – life's organic activities are more than the motion of atoms – one enacts a different science with appropriate concepts and laws that conform to the specific subject matter.

This clarification is necessary in order to avoid the temptation of judging all valid sciences as only subdivisions of physics or broad imitations thereof. The scientific enterprise is not a one-dimensional way of knowing things. It must take into consideration the precise differences in the subject matter under study. Reality is too diverse in its evidence to allow a single perspective to exhaust its riches. Genuine knowledge requires differing perspectives, approaches and methodologies, and the investigator will employ different language terms to reflect his findings.

The study of human consciousness as a living awareness uses the special methodology of introspection. Thus its procedures and results will differ from the quantitative expectations obtained in the physical sciences.

Before outlining the meditation experiment in broad strokes, let us begin with some preliminary fact-finding at the common sense level. Here ordinary introspection and reflection on everyday experiences will suffice for our purposes. Later, introspection will be used formally as a procedural tool throughout the experiment. But the investigator will refine its application as he probes further into the experiment.

In a normal day, one notices that the mind and body undergo various kinds of change. Endless thoughts and images occupy one's attention. Countless sensations and feelings stimulate the body. The meditator, like everyone else, experiences almost relentless alteration in mood. During a twenty-four hour period, neither the mind nor the body would seem to qualify as invariant constants eligible for an experiment. Both are changing their condition too randomly to allow for any consistency in results.

Where does that leave the possibility of an experiment? What else remains for the investigator/meditator to study but his body and mind? The question is whether the body-mind complex in its variable moods can demonstrate sufficient stability for prolonged study.

Granted that the body and the mind fluctuate throughout the day, everyone still feels and thinks that he is always, in some vague fundamental way, the same individual who undergoes these recurring changes. A typical day may find one in different locales, weather conditions, and social surroundings. The range of episodes on any typical day are unpredictable as well as unlimited in their diversity. The variety of intellectual and sensual experiences occur to the same person.

Like seasons, our moods change and alter their colour periodically, yet always one senses continuity within oneself. Whether one experiences life as a series of fluid configurations or a stack of contiguous snapshots, something abides that, in spite of the unpredictable and often illogical occurrences that blur into each other, renders continuity to these episodes. Life is not a quilt of experiences seamed together by the incidental threads of time, space and location, but a continuing panorama that engages the self-same witness. While waking, dreaming and sleeping may comprise my apparent range of notable experiences, in between these traveled states I do not suffer annihilation. Somehow, something accounts for my sense of oneness throughout these experiences. Something about me sustains its existence without changing amidst the changes experienced. Without some perdurable, underlying reality upon which these mental and bodily changes take place, change itself is impossible. Change cannot exist by and in itself; any change occurs or takes place in an existing reality. Thus, throughout all the changes in my physical, mental and emotional makeup, the same "I" persists as the individual experiencer.

Given this brief review of the human experience of mood changes, let us now state the hypothesis that will be applied to the subject matter, namely, the fluctuating consciousness of the investigator. The hypothesis, then, is that the investigator will first proceed to investigate his own consciousness, noting its changes, and by applying throughout the investigation the appropriate method will discover a stable order of reality that prevails universally among human beings. Secondly, the more the investigator performs this experiment, the more he will grasp the nature of consciousness, which knowledge will provide increasing control over its use. This entire experimental process is called meditation.

The hypothesis is then carried out, or tested, by carefully setting up the conditions for the experiment in the recommended manner. A stationary posture is assumed, eyes are closed, and rhythmic breathing commences. The coordination of the procedure gradually eliminates the disturbing sensual impressions and subdues the fluctuating images and concepts. A systematic process is undergone by the experimenter who attentively directs, controls and observes the self-induced experiment. The relaxed stationary posture settles the body and the rhythmic breathing settles the nervous system while calming the imagination. The experimenter gradually focuses his inner attention in a designated manner that permits him to witness the entire quieting process. As the interiorization of his concentration lingers, the latent sensitivity of his consciousness intensifies. As the experiment is repeated daily, duplicating the sequence of steps, further self-awareness occurs as the experimenter refines the process. Repeated experiments yield more knowledge and the eventual power of control over the mind and its variables.

Through first-hand exposure the experimenter/meditator

now knows that he is not his mental variables, that he is surpass-ingly more than his thoughts and feelings, more than the customary states of consciousness that occupy his normal hours. By investigating meditation, he investigates himself; by investi-gating himself, he discovers the perdurable factor which not only gives continuity to life's experiences, but also remains intact through all personality changes. In the experiment of meditating, the investigator/meditator discovers the basic constant: the unchanging presence of his consciousness.

This discovery is not a private, isolated event. Samplings of various other subject–meditators would concur with similar findings. The personal insight derived from the experiment expands into universal knowledge about human nature. With continual exposures to the method, the experimenter eventually discovers that the dynamic constant of consciousness is the sole source that accounts for personality changes. The complex of values, attitudes, and behaviour that distinguishes people in similar or different circumstances can now be traced to the dynamics of this constant.

During the day, as well as in meditation, the mind processes various kinds of sense impressions and concepts. The mind assumes this content from the outside world or retrieves it from memory. Because of one's goals and tasks with life, it is helpful to build certain habits of interpreting life. The mind becomes fond of its mental habits – its ways of evaluating, judging and expressing. The problem is not that these habits are good or bad, practical or nonsensical. Rather these mental determi-nations may be preventing the meditator from increasing his understanding and enjoyment of life. A dependency grows for certain thought patterns or responses that constrain the mind to look at life from fixed points of view. One hardly realizes how closely consciousness has aligned itself with its habitual stances. But persisting in meditation, one slowly recognizes that the fondness for these habits of perception and judgement may be useful but they are also definitely limiting.

The mental fluctuations and contents of the day, new and old, are the variables that need inner control. These mental modifications (called *vrittis* in yoga philosophy) are appraised through the use of discernment (*viveka*). The act of meditation enlarges one's self-awareness of how the mind becomes enamored by its contents and with this insight, a rebalancing can ensue. The meditator now sees where he was dependent upon his limited mental outlook as the only way to appreciate life, rather than using his mental apparatus freely in the world. He was thus paving his own road of suffering (*klesas*).

Meditation, we now see, is the experimental science of human consciousness. Everything one does, feels, wishes or imagines is possible because consciousness is the underlying reality. Meditation is not a science of thinking; the reasoning realm is only one of its descernible levels. As a process of interiorization, meditative investigation proceeds beyond the margins of thought into the regions of creative intuition, exploring the full range of consciousness.

Clues emerge during daily experimentation which vindicate the experiment: increased tranquility, smoother coordination of body and mind, less tension, more relaxed sleep, among others. These results or signs indicate that the experimenter is proceeding properly. Moreover, the systematic practice gives one a sense of reassurance that the science is not hit or miss.

When the methodology, the interior experimentation of meditation, proceeds in this orderly manner, definite qualitative results can be verified. Both in its method of investigation and in the results of its procedure, meditation is a special type of science. The goal or truth of meditation is not speculative information but a transformative knowledge. In discovering the chemical contents of the human brain, for example, my behaviour is unaffected; in discovering the nature of the mind through meditation, the power to change behaviour is mine to express. Meditation is thus a practical science: it transforms the investigator during his act of investigating. At the practical, everyday level of jostling with life, one learns through meditation that the seeds of happiness are sown within, and by nourishing them a bridge is built to intelligent living in the outside world.

CHAPTER 7

The Meaning of Revelation

Sacred scriptures, if they have meaning, must reveal that meaning in our lives today. To read the Torah for inspiration at the moment, for example, indicates that the reader assumes the life and law of Moses has value for modern living. Likewise, for a Christian to read a letter of St Paul assumes that the contents pertain in some way to the twentieth century as well as to the first.

People revere sacred scriptures not just for their historical significance, but especially for their personal significance. The value of scriptures is their universal import. They can affect people in different cultures at varying periods of history. Not every passage in scripture necessarily inspires in the same way, however. Consequently the problem of interpretation accompanies the endeavor to understand revelation.

This chapter will explore the problem of interpreting revelation by first discussing the composition of scripture, and second, how to approach interpretation as a tool for understanding scripture. To aid this approach, the contribution of yoga practices is explained.

The Nature of Revelation

One speaks of the Bible or any scripture as a revelation. Truth has been revealed. These revealed truths have such a stature because they are meant to guide people in understanding the ultimate meaning of life. To communicate universal truths requires a dexterity of expression. The versatility of genre often found in scripture would indicate that transcendental truths can, and indeed must, have more than a single articulation. The Judaic-Christian scriptures are a typical example.

As a written account of more than three thousand years of accumulated revelation, the Bible is more like a library in many volumes than a single work. As a compilation of legends, parables, aphorisms, songs, sagas, poetry, sermons, legislation, historical documents, epics, liturgical rules and quotations, these writings offer a mixture of literary genre to say the least.

The various types of writings indicate different authors and editors, most of whom have remained anonymous. The biblical languages do not easily lend themselves to abstract concepts and resemble the everyday graphic changeableness of nature. More concrete than abstract, more fluid than fixed, these ancient languages possess those qualities of imagery that writers delight in – enigmas, figures of speech and play on words. Their reverence for holy writ did not prevent them from taking advantage of every occasion.

The story of Samson in the Book of Judges illustrates a typical episode that had become an exaggerated legend. Samson's exploits are really war stories suitable for stirring the morale of the Israelites in their battles with the Philistines. The famous scene where he survives an attack of a thousand men by using the jawbone of an ass for his weapon and later throwing it away is an amusing tale. It relies upon the reader's appreciation of puns. The name of the hill upon which this incredible victory took place was called Leki, which means "jawbone". When reading the story in Judges 15: 9–17 one also must remember that the word "hill" in Hebrew is pronounced in the same way as the word for "to throw away".

The exploits of the great King David are likewise immodestly embellished. In 1 Samuel 17:4–54 we read the story of how young David killed the giant Goliath with a smooth stone flung from his sling shot. In another book, 2 Samuel 21:19–21 we read that "Elhanan son of Jair from Bethlehem killed Goliath of Gath", and that in another battle "there was a man of huge stature with six fingers on each hand and six toes on each foot . . . and Jonathan, son of David's brother, Shimeah, killed him when he defied Israel". Obviously, both David and two other warriors could not single-handedly be responsible for Goliath's death. This contradiction may be partially explained by remembering that the Bible is a series of traditions blended together. Some of the traditions overlap with others and repeat the same episodes. The scholars seem to think that David's reputation as the slayer of Goliath is a nice war story that is not credible. The Book of Chronicles, which is a magnificent whitewash of David's shadow side, does not even place him at the battle with the Philistines.

To interpret the text in a literal way is correct provided the reader has the literal meaning intended by the author. But to read the text with the surface literalness of a weather report can place the sincere reader in embarrassing positions. In this regard, how many believers of the Bible follow its injunction to become vegetarians? "God said, 'see I give you all the seed-bearing plants that are upon the earth, and all the trees with seed-bearing fruit; this shall be your food' ". (Genesis 1:29).

An easy example of literalness is Jesus' warning about the rich man and the camel passing through the eye of a needle. "It is easier for a camel to pass through the eye of a needle than for a rich man to enter the kingdom of God". (Matthew 19:24). Passageways into the major cities of Israel were frequently given names. The Needle's Eye was the gate used by travellers and merchants. Thus we understand Jesus' image of the overburdened camel attempting to squeeze through the small toll gate of the city. A bit of geographical background and cultural information makes a world of difference from taking the text at face value.

The Bible, like every sacred scripture, nevertheless is a second-hand exposition. The experiences recounted in the biblical writings are the fundamental revelation. From a careful reading one begins to gain insight into the biblical meaning.

Due to the various authors and the circumstances that called forth the writings, the Bible offers a range of meanings. It challenges readers because its authors wrote from various depths of meaning. Dante, in his *Divine Comedy* summarized the levels of meaning that Christian theologians and meditators had discovered over the centuries pondering the riches of the texts. He mentions:

> The scriptures can be understood, and ought to be explained principally in four senses. One is called literal . . . the second is called allegorical . . . the third sense is called moral . . . the fourth sense is called anagogical, that is, beyond sense; and this is when a scripture is spiritually expounded, which while true in its literal sense, refers beyond it to the higher things of the Eternal Glory. . . . [1]

The Bible is written, as the Fathers of the Church and medievalists knew, for various levels of understanding. Taking only one perspective on the scripture, reading everything from only one point of view, surrounds the reader with inconsistencies and contradictions that are unexplainable on a word for word basis.

The complexity of the scriptures is there because the author is inspired, attempting to transpose a revelation, that is, an experience of divine origin, into human language on paper. What greater disproportion could there be than to reduce a transcendental event to a few hundred human words? At this point the problem of expression contains two factors to reconcile: revelation and communication.

Treating a sacred event with the tools of language, finding the images and phrases that convey its divine origin, preserving the right context of meaning for the benefit of the listener to make contact with the word of God, are all the pressured concerns of the writer. When God speaks to man in a single word, it takes man 10,000 words to explain it to others. The experiencer wants to communicate the liberating event of revelation to others. How? To the former factors of expression must now be added symbolization and participation.

The only adequate way to describe the latent possibilities of scripture for various levels of authentic meaning is to recognize the flexible character of the sacred texts. Next to the revelatory experience itself – Moses before the burning bush, Jesus in the bright light at the top of Mount Tabor, the disciples awaiting the breath of the Spirit in the form of fire – the closest second-hand approximation is the effort to convey the event through symbolization.

The complex truths of scriptures reveal a realm of reality, exceedingly intelligible, but disclosed by neither the senses nor discursive reason. The normal faculties for contacting the world at large are limited when it comes to the apprehension of divine truths. A sensible and rational rendering of the Bible can yield positive results. As Dante reminds us, however, there are significances unrevealed by rational investigation.

Allegorical and moral significance are present in the texts. These levels of meaning require a certain finesse on the part of the reader, a certain sympathy or feeling for what the author intends. People who respect and strive for a virtuous life, for example, will discover the moral aphorisms pervading many passages. The Bible can serve as an uplifting source of inner nourishment for mind and heart. The texts, even at an elementary level, propose answers and questions asked by everyone. Matters of creation, the beginning of evil, human destiny, the careers of sages and saints, are touched upon throughout the Bible.

From the biblical text itself, assertions and overtones point out that there is more to scripture than the texts narrate. There are statements that leave the reader perplexed. What does saying, "the kingdom is within" have to do with my human nature? How does a modern person square scientific facts with scenes of power that exceed the normal course of action (the miracles)?

Can a modern believer duplicate the feats attributed to the followers of Jesus?

The Bible states these unusual events without explaining them. The inability to answer the natural questions prompted by a fair reading of the texts has led to placing these suprahuman demonstrations outside the reach of normal human attainment. The disproportion between the event of revelation and the limitations of words may unfairly move the average reader to underestimate his human potentials.

Revelation uses natural descriptions but the written word contains flashes of meaning that the unwary reader may easily miss. No amount of exegetical language study will suffice for unlocking these meanings. Many passages in scripture are truly not for the unprepared, the sincere believer who nevertheless does not possess the qualifications of discernment.

The tools for the literal meaning are different from the qualifications for the moral level. These levels are not interchangeable, although the second depends upon the first. Revelation in itself signifies an unveiling of divine origins. This experience takes outward shape for communication's sake in oral and written forms. Regardless of how ecstatic an experience may be, if I wish to communicate it to a stranger I am forced to address him to a great extent on his home ground. Otherwise no communication takes place. So also the Bible has to use words that convey divine reality. Therefore symbol is used.

Symbolic language implies more than words or their intellectual contents. A symbol is intelligible and meaningful to everyday life, without necessarily being rationally comprehended in all its aspects. One may speak of a courageous human, for example, as having a "lion's heart." Many nations have selected the eagle as their national symbol of power and government. In both instances, the symbolic meaning is more than just the reference to an animal and a bird as such. The symbol may require sufficient moral and intellectual preparation to ready one, as it were, to pierce the veiled truth.

The symbol's power resides in its ability to evoke hidden realities. In the very act of contacting the symbol, the mind knows only partially the significance of the represented reality. The symbolic reality opens to a different kind of exegesis. This exegesis is the direct product of the writer's state of consciousness. The significance of the writer's vision is best appreciated by the reader whose mind is at the same level. Then the symbols make sense. The biblical sages illustrate this well.

The enrichment of the biblical insight, learning the message, requires more than academic qualifications. Sacred scripture is meant not to inform the reader about historical events but to touch the reader's life in a profound way. This kind of communication is not just the result of reading the words. At this juncture, the discipline of yoga can play an important role for biblical interpretation.

The practical import of yoga is the evolution of awareness. One becomes more adept at understanding the meaning of life, not as a result of information or additional concepts, but as a growth in awareness through the transformation of an individual's conscious life force. There is a certain relationship here. The more one stimulates the life force, the more one becomes receptive. The actual power to grasp the meaning of life and be transformed by that meaning is available through the practice of yoga. Since yoga affects the mind–body relationship, it cannot but help one in understanding sacred scripture.

As we have seen in a previous chapter, the five *yamas* and the five *niyamas* are foundational commitments that dispose the student for receptivity. These guidelines can produce a qualitative alteration in one's character that improves the art of biblical interpretation. A new integration of the vital dimensions arises as one progresses in *raja* yoga. Yoga especially concerns itself with improving the range and quality of human awareness. The power or capacity to apprehend meanings is, over time, greatly affected. In this way the reader's mind is prepared to be more sensitive to the richer meanings contained in biblical scenes. There is a kind of internal purification that stimulates the power of the mind to penetrate the mystery that life in itself reveals and that the Bible clarifies. The depth of biblical interpretation flows from the depths of consciousness.

The lives of the prophets show an unusual degree of consciousness. Either they were strangely hallucinating or they gave remarkable evidence of power over nature and insight into man's practical problems. They spoke in a manner that conveyed to their audience an inner vision that few recognized for themselves but many respected as genuinely important. Their performance emanated from a higher state of consciousness than their listening contemporaries. Their inner vision abided in their lives and continued to influence their judgments, often at the expense of seemingly more rational solutions protested by their neighbors.

While the Bible endorses a positive view of man's sublime nature, it does not supply the detailed steps to its full realization. The early commentators of the Bible, however, the laity and recluses of the Christian communities of the Egyptian, Northern Indian and Palestinian regions, demonstrate in their writings a type of exegesis that directly contends with reaching the cosmic event.

The type of exegesis that allows for the final resolution of biblical symbol is direct participation in the reality symbolized. The kingdom being within, one enters within to discover it. Scripture reveals in symbolic instances those truths that are fully recognized only in the inner experience of spirit. The final level of exegesis is the individual's disciplined process of inspiration: one's spirit enters into itself consciously, thereby experiencing self-revelation. Inspired, literally filled with the spirit, all modes and degrees of the scriptural meanings become transparent. Inspiration becomes revelation – the same experience. One crosses the border of time into the cosmic event. The inner experience transforms consciousness into cosmic universality, wherein individual relative truths, heretofore discovered and entertained by the rational faculty at its best, pale in comparison. Like the Apostles, one becomes an "eyewitness." The scriptures are sacred because the authors' conscious projections of their own illumined state reveal in symbolic fashion the divine significance of life. The mystery of Christ-consciousness does not belong to the dead past; biblical truth is not admired only in faith. Like John on the island of Patmos, one has only to enter into his own spirit to reveal the cosmic mystery of the Bible.

CHAPTER 8

Naming God

In any society there are social symbols that function as a unifying element. A country's flag, the mention of a hero's name, the recall of a catastrophic event, can all exert an influence upon individuals or rally a community to action. Group memories and associations have a dramatic impact on people's lives. These experiences are preserved, utilized and summarized by most communities as a source of their identity. This ability to depict experiences of great value, to forge symbols, is found throughout cultures and history.

Among Christians of every denomination, the use of religious language has been a source of identity and thus a bond of unity for believers. One of the most important symbols, if not the most crucial one, within any church community is the concept of God. The importance of this symbol among all Christians is its key position in their minds for justifying and unifying everything else about their beliefs and morals. The symbol "God" functions as the foundational belief and provides believers with their understanding of the meaning of life and death.

To appreciate the importance of symbols in society, however, as well as in religion, interpretation is required. Symbols derive their power from interpretation. Unless one interprets reality, life remains meaningless; with interpretation, life yields meaning. Without meaning one stands mute before the reality in question. Nothing transpires.

In interpretation one deciphers the intelligibility of something – an action, a word, an idea – and arrives at a meaning about it. If my foreign friend has never seen a professional baseball game, it becomes my job to explain or decipher for him the symbols of the game – those actions and words used in the event, and without which the game can be neither understood nor enjoyed.

The marvelous quality of interpretation is that it can be conveyed to others. Meaning can be structured and transferred through symbols. Thus, communication takes place. In ordinary circumstances, the symbols of language work because they convey meanings. Normal conversation occurs not through sounds impinging upon the nervous system and brain but primarily through the exchange of meanings. The question "why" that the child repeats incessantly is another way of saying, "What does it mean"? Unless the sounds of words bear meaning, no interpretation is available. No communication results. Words are intelligible only because they are meaningful sounds.

Our lives are full of symbols. Man himself is the most symbolic of realities. Our conversation, our dress, our walk, our job, our leisure moments, our religion have meaning if only for ourselves. What we think, say and do possesses meaning because these activities are real. Since reality is the basis for meaning, what does not exist in some way has no meaning. My imagined thoughts, however, do have meaning since they are products of my real imagination, even though there is no reference to reality outside my mind.

Meanings are expressed in symbols. To speak of a blue sky to a person blind from birth is meaningless. There is no experience of the reality with which to connect the two words. The symbolic utterance of these words, while meaningful to most people, remains empty of significance to a sightless person.

I understand something because I can refer the explanation to my experience of the reality. To understand something presupposes my experience of it. People often emphasize the importance of their announcement by saying, "I speak from experience". The understanding or explanation is then cast into symbols. The symbol in turn derives its meaning from the "felt" experience. In this way we make life intelligible to ourselves and articulate it to others.

The accepted ways people use symbols in society apply to those experiences in which they recognize or interpret the same meaning. Symbols communicate meaning to the extent that the community shares in a common experience. As a citizen, or member of a community, I know what you mean when you speak about something because I, like yourself, have some experience regarding the subject discussed. Ordinary human intercourse means that the participants understand each other's use of symbols, having experienced the feeling of their meaning.

The Symbol God

The formative factors that have produced and are producing Western culture are not necessarily reinforcing the traditional beliefs in God. In fact, cultural life today mitigates the possibility of believing in God. This state of affairs does not imply a subtle and far-reaching atheistic plot against institutional Christianity; the phenomenon simply exists. There are discernible causes for this reduction of belief in God, but we will focus instead on examining the crisis for any positive signs of religious vitality.

In a society that assumes newness and progress as basic to cultural survival, it should not come as a surprise that religious concepts change. Is it possible that a closer look at the symbol God as it occurs in our changing culture may reveal flaws?

The meaning of God as learned from religion classes and theology manuals may show a significance on paper, but there the relevance ends. In the factual condition of life today, this theoretic significance may be utterly unconnected to the daily struggles and ambitions of society. Theoretical coherence is not enough. The symbol God stands for ultimate and practical significance or it is not worth the time for consideration. To place this symbol into the market place, amidst the mass of factors shaping cultural life, demands a test for its applicability. Will belief in God stand up against life as it is experienced?

People are not so much doubting God's existence as they are God's meaning. For most people higher values that transcend the corrosion of time are a necessity for a meaningful life. But in attempting to articulate these higher values, they are seriously looking at alternative options to the institutional concept or presentation of God. While every religion has its own portrait of God, the elaboration of the symbol must somehow relate to human experience. Without this descernible reference to life as it is encountered, God remains an abstraction. If the symbol God stands for the completeness of life, the removal of privation and suffering, then asserting the symbol should do just that: complete life and remove suffering. It should achieve what it symbolizes.

Here, it seems to me, is the crux of the issue. Are religious symbols, especially that of God, realizable for people in their daily lives? Since God is the most comprehensible symbol in which one could believe, the activation of belief in that symbol should have comprehensive effects upon the life of the believer.

When human life is not being transformed by this most ultimate symbol known to civilization, there are basically only two reasons for that default. First, the believer is not engaging the symbol properly, somewhat like the child who reported to his parents that God is a "green bean". Upon checking the information the parents discovered that the teacher referred to God as a "supreme being". While the implications of viewing God as a legume have never been documented, the failure of the symbol, in this instance, lies with the believer.

In addition to not being able to grasp the symbol of divinity correctly, there is a second, more crucial default. What if the symbol itself is incorrect? *God* in English is a three-lettered word; the Latin, *Deos*, is four-lettered; the Greek, *Theos*, is five-lettered; the Hebrew, *El*, is two-lettered. By themselves as combinations of four different alphabets, these words are arbitrary. There is nothing sacrosanct in using just these letters. The letters forming the name God in the mind mean different things to different people. The religions have chosen (interpreted) the contents of the word God. The God of the Calvinists is not the God of the Roman Catholics, nor is the God of the Lutherans the same as the God of Orthodox Jews. When yoga texts refer to *Ishwara*, likewise translated as God, this designation means something very different from the denominational concept of the Christian notion of God. What makes the difference is not the name but the meaning of the name.

The next question is, where did the meanings come from? The plural meanings of God prevailing today among believers may not be due only to the various denominational interpretations of God. Overlooked frequently is a prior consideration which affects the very construction of a symbol: the human mind.

While people speak and act symbolically, it is only their mind that catches the meanings contained in symbols. Without consciousness, there are no symbols expressed or apprehended. The construction of a symbol like God, however, puts a task upon the mind that is not required in everyday communication. The environment, for example, is sensibly and intelligibly available to neighbors. Public availability allows for a shared experience of life that is immediately referable for anyone's scrutiny. Words have a local character because the community uses them that way. When one lives in a region, one learns what they mean. This public availability allows even strangers eventually to grasp the meaning of things. The public availability to meaning can be experienced directly and immediately. Local symbols become commonplace.

The Name for God

God is a different story. The criteria of public availability does not exist for apprehending the meaning of God. Neither Church, synagogue, creed, liturgy nor Bible makes God knowable to the mind. In dealing with the God symbol, the mind is taking on a necessary task that ironically exceeds it. The power of rationality tends to rely upon sensory images for conceiving its symbols. The images and concepts of the mind are drawn from our experience of daily living. We can invent new arrangements in our minds but these arrangements still use the same images and ideas drawn from life's experiences. It is exactly like designing a patchwork quilt. The patches of cloth can be arranged into many patterns, but each design uses the same patches.

A further dilemma looms. How can we compose a symbol when there seems to be no obvious grounding for it? Preaching the symbol does not explain it, but only enforces it through emotion. The problem of whether this symbolic version of God is meaningful remains unanswered.

Today people are reluctant to assume the truth of religious statements because of authoritative force. It is not a resistance generated by anarchy, but a critical attitude that recognizes the inherent limitations of the mind. For Jews, Christians, and Mohammedans to insist that their symbol of God is the only acceptable one, would be similar to producing a textbook on world geography that contained only maps of Jerusalem, Rome and Mecca.

Any symbol of God is like a sandpail into which one tries to pour the ocean. The pail holds some water but it does not hold the ocean. When one holds onto his idea of God as the last word he has made the pail equivalent to the ocean.

It may seem unfair, but every symbol of God involves a necessary illusion. The mind easily identifies its constructs with the reality that they represent. Wars have been fought over whose God is supreme. It is quite customary to assume that one's idea of God is the finest expression, the final word, on this sacred reality. In so doing, however, one succumbs to a deadly trap that the prophets of the Old Testament repeatedly warned their people against. The assumption that your concrete word is the exclusive symbol that designates God is idolatry. An idea about the sacred becomes an idol, an illusion, when we misidentify it as being the reality.

The believer's effort to portray God in concepts and images cannot be avoided. How else would there be communication? But if there is one universal agreement among all spiritual traditions it is the declaration that the ultimate origin of the universe is beyond a detailed description. If God does not exceed the range of human images and concepts, then man makes God into his own image and thus worships an idol of his own construction.

There is an unresolvable tension in attempting to name divinity. The divine origin of life and the universe, on the one hand, is incomprehensible, while man's mind, on the other hand, deals with finite realities. The riddle of existence exceeds man's rational mind because it possesses too much intelligibility for man to grasp. The discursive mind grasps things in bits and pieces. Human learning takes place in steps. We can see this in the fact that although modern societies are run on electricity, no scientist is bold enough to assert that he has the complete story on electro-magnetism. If the world at large presents challenges to our knowing it, how much more does its divine author?

Since human experience on a day-to-day basis constantly deals with finite, changing things, how does one even imagine an infinite, eternal reality? It is true that philosophers and theologians speak of divine attributes like infinity, omniscience, omnipresence, eternal in their description of God. But what do these terms mean in their minds when their world of experiences is just the opposite of these attributes?

The Bible offers a plentitude of attempts to describe God:

I am that I am (Exodus 3/14)
Fair (Psalms: 27/4)
God of gods and Lord of lords (Psalms:136/2,3)

Eternal (Deuteronomy: 33/27)
Giver of life (Genesis: 1/20)
Holy of holies (Isiah: 6/3)
Wisdom (Proverbs: 8)
Wrathful (Psalms: 88/16)
Surpassing all things in greatness (Isiah: 40/15)

Biblical writers also declare God in poetic, anthropomorphic and nature terms. God is referred to as:

A star (Revelations: 22/16)
Fire (Deuteronomy: 4.24)
Sun (Psalms: 84/11)
Water (Psalms: 84/6)
Wind (John: 4/24)
Cloud (Exodus: 13/21)
Dew (Hosea: 14/5)
A still breeze (1 Kings: 19/12)
A stone (Psalms: 118/22)
Father (John: 20/17)
Mystery (Daniel: 2ff)
A Lion (Hosea: 11/10)
Mother (Isiah: 66/13)

These different names apply depending upon what portion of the Bible one reads. Yet no tradition within the Judaic-Christian Bible would claim that its presentation of God is utterly adequate. There is no symbol in these scriptures that adequately portrays the totality of God's meaning. God remains the *mysterium tremendum*, the "awesome mystery" that defies conceptualization.

If one goes outside the Bible and examines even older scriptures, the same descriptions are found. In the *Vedas*, ten-thousand-year-old scriptures, one reads:

Exceedingly wise, exceedingly strong is the Designer.
He is creator, disposer, epiphany supreme.
He is our Father who begot us, he the Disposer
who knows all situations, every creature. (Rig Veda: 10/82)

The Inspirer of all men advances, the Sun,
displaying his mighty shimmering banner. (Rig Veda:
7/63)

He who is called Divine Friend brings men together.
The Divine Friend supports both earth and heaven,
watching over people, never closing an eye. (Rig Veda:
3/59,1)

Behold the marvelous mystery of God.
Near though he is, one cannot leave him.
Near though he is, one cannot see him.
He does not die, nor does he grow old. (Atharve Veda:
10/8/32)

In the Bhagavad Gita we read:

I am the sacrifice and the offering, the sacred gift and the
sacred plant. I am the holy words, the holy food, the holy
fire, and the offering that is made in the fire. (Bhagavad
Gita: 9/16)

Consider my sacred mystery: I am the source of all beings,
I support them all, but I rest not in them. Even as the
mighty winds rest in the vastness of the ethereal space, all
beings have their rest in me. Through my nature I bring

forth all creation, and this rolls around in the circles of time,
but I am not bound by this vast work of creation. I am
and I watch the drama of works. (Bhagavad Gita: 9/5–9)

Quite literally, there are few descriptions in the Bible that cannot be found in other world scriptures referring to the divine
reality. The Hewbrews and Christians were neither the exclusive
nor the first composers of their revered symbols. Compiling all
the symbols in both traditions that refer to God would still not
add up to disclosing the full meaning of the eternal reality. Due
to the limitations of any symbol, there can hardly be an ideal
symbol for God. The meaning of symbol as symbol indicates
that the mind recognizes there is always more to the referent
than the reference tells. One suspects a surplus meaning that
still needs further elaboration. If we overlook the surplus, then
we easily assume that our symbol is the complete one.

Unless the believer who searches for divine symbols recalls
that there is more than his conceptualization, then he partakes
of an illusion. If he is sure of the total meaning of God, then
he represses all other possibilities. No substitutes are acceptable.
There looms, then, the implicit danger that the believer believes
too much. The God symbol becomes a ruse for its possessor.
We often invent symbols that possess a meaning that is total,
precisely because we invented the meaning. For instance, the
design of a computer program possesses only that meaning
which the programmer puts into it. The divine reality, however,
is *totaliter aliter* – wholly other than any symbol that could ever
be invented.

Attempting divine symbols would then seem an impossible
task. Are there any guides, remote or otherwise, to render clues
to knowing divine reality? In religious language and theological
statements, one might use an ancient principle, namely, that
one should never expect more clarity and certainty than the
subject matter allows. At the same time, there is a coefficient
factor that accompanies the principle: one cannot make music

more beautiful than the instrument permits. Human subjectivity enters into all our efforts to be objective. What appeals to us about the God symbol learned at Sunday school may later become peripheral as we mature into life. The composition of our religious symbols should reflect our struggles with uncovering meaning in life. The stories in the Bible are packed with this diversified approach to God. As we grow up we assume uncritically many ideas and feelings about our environment, people and destiny. Our cherished notions about divine realities are not insulated against this growth process. We subtract and we add to the meaning of life. Even with an intelligent and conscientious respect for life, certain meanings about reality do not show up until the time is ripe. Ripening is usually a lengthy and uneven process of struggling with life's experiences. What someone grasps in the symbol of God as a single adult, is not a duplication of his religious thoughts in childhood, and even further from his thoughts of God after becoming a parent. Rival notions of God could hardly not be expected in society.

How strange to find in the Old Testament a gross and brutal characterization of God that inspired Moses' followers to pillage and rape the promised land in his name:

> Why have you spared the life of all the women? . . . Kill all the male children, kill also all the women who have slept with a man. Spare the lives only of the young girls who have not slept with a man and take them for yourselves . . . This is a statute of the law which Yahweh has commanded Moses (Numbers 31:15ff).

Later we listen to the prophet Isaiah describe a God of irrevocable love and tenderness for all creatures:

> Now your creator will be your husband . . . Yes, like a forsaken wife, distressed in spirit, Yahweh calls you back.

Does a man cast off the wife of his youth? says your God.
I did forsake you for a brief moment, but with great love
will I take you back (Isiah 54:5,6).

If the Hebrews had settled for their initial attempts to fathom the
meaning of God then scripture would not have gotten beyond
portraying God as a tribal warrior.

The multitude of symbols found in the scripture suggests the
varied attempts of man to overcome the limitations of his mind
in discovering and expressing the meaning of God. The narratives that name God in scripture never tell the reader why that
particular symbol is used. The symbols that relate to the natural
surroundings and events of the time are an interpretation. Those
of us who examine the Bible today are therefore obligated to
interpret an interpretation. One's familiarity with nature and
history is presupposed in order to appreciate the corresponding
symbols describing God. Our growth through life's experiences
make it a necessity for reinterpreting again and again, if
necessary, the ultimate meaning of existence.

God symbols have to be inexact, indirect and unfinished,
subject to revision, since they reflect the stages of our self-
understanding. The need for reinterpretation is a safety measure
against the smug complacency of those who have God, like life,
all figured out. Even the disruptions of life can awaken the
interpretive opportunity for knowing the ultimate mystery a
little better.

Descriptions of God from varied spiritual traditions are to
our benefit. They preserve the mind's suppleness. We recognize
that although genuine symbols insinuate the divine reality, they
cannot contain the holy other. By examining the multi directions of these symbols, we stand a better chance of correcting
our superstitions and clarifying the meaning of life's destiny.
"But there are some great souls who know me. Their refuge is
my own divine nature. They love me with a oneness of love;
they know that I am the source of all" (Bhagavad Gita 9:13).

Chapter 9

The Master-Disciple Tradition

Since the Christian tradition encompasses a 2000-year-old history, it should not be surprising that there are many things in the tradition that are not remembered today. Among the forgotten truths of Christianity is the fundamental relationship that Jesus developed with his close followers. It is the Eastern relationship of master and disciple. Unknown in Western culture, a modern reader misses this relationship in the biblical scenes. In the West we read the biblical narratives that use terms like master, Lord, disciple, apostle, without always realizing their significance in their day. Nowhere in theological writings nor in the religious mentality of typical Christians does one find an appreciation for the apprenticeship of master and disciple.

By inspecting the cultural meaning of the Gospel words in their textual use, one can hopefully gain an important understanding for our times.

Christian Faith: The Prerogative of God

Christian denominations seriously foster a tradition of communicating religious content to their converts. And yet every denomination exhibits an ambivalence toward communication. On the one hand, churches express their religious concern for proper indoctrination. On the other, those chiefly responsible for instruction – the minister, priests, nuns, teachers, parents – are the first to admit that the principal and exclusive agent for communicating faith is God. Only God gives the gift of conversion. Only God draws man to Himself though faith. People hear the biblical word and are moved by the divine gift of faith. It is God who somehow, mysteriously, disposes the recipient for belief. God remains sovereignly free, transcendent to human pressure or solicitation. Understandably, then, Christians view themselves as the receivers of God's good will, totally dependent upon that will prevailing. One is left with the impression that the disposal of faith remains entirely God's responsibility.

The failing of this kind of religious communication is that it makes no real allowance for human participation. If God does what he will, then why should those authorities responsible for religious indoctrination be conscientious? In the context that God's grace is all, the role of the religious educator would barely exist. This emphasis upon God's sole agency questions the necessity of a human teacher as well as the active participation of the convert. The serious reduction of the human agency makes of faith an instantaneous, magical force in the recipient. The human teacher and the aspirant would play utterly receptive roles. Only God, in other words, produces the miracles of making that alteration in human consciousness called faith.

It is this typical faith model of God as active agent and the believer as passive recipient that needs examination. When this model of religious communication between God and a potential believer is transposed to the Gospels, Jesus becomes the active teacher and the disciples are the passive believers.

The Meaning of Apprenticeship

In the New Testament there are many scenes that involve Jesus' role as teacher to his followers. The believers that Jesus chose to instruct are given a specific designation: the Greek word, *mathetes*, or disciple, which is used 197 times. We are familiar with the words 'disciple' and 'master' as these words appear in the English translations of the Greek Bible. Yet we have little use for the word master in English today. Master of the house or master teacher are anachronisms in Western culture. In the East, however, the term master persists. There, one can legitimately refer to qualified individuals as master artists, masters in martial arts or spiritual masters. This notion of master is quite common in the Middle East as well. Jewish rabbis, for example, have always been known as masters.

The concrete meaning of master (Greek, *didaskelos*) conveys more than competence in a field of art or learning. When used with the word *didaskein*, to apprentice, it appears 49 times in the Gospels and implies a special relationship with students. Throughout the biblical texts when Jesus is referred to as master with his student disciples, the word *didaskein* is always employed. Unfortunately the rich meaning of the Greek does not come through in the English text. The English often translates the Greek by the word "teaches", which does not convey the meaning of apprenticeship. It is true that the function of *didaskein* is teaching, but our twentieth-century use of the word does not capture the impact of its use in its original context.

When a master chooses to accept someone as a student, that person commits himself and his lifestyle to the requirements of the master. This profound relationship between master and disciple has nothing to do with registering for courses and attending formal classes. As much as possible, the relationship becomes a daily, lived association. The disciple is a disciple only because he apprentices to the master. The British use of apprenticeship approaches, but does not convey the intensity of the Eastern notion.

Biblically, to be called a disciple (*mathetes*), means that one apprentices (*didaskein*) to a master (*didaskelos*). This relationship implies much more than our fondest memories of a teacher-student episode in high school or college. Apprenticeship is more akin to the rapport between parent and child, where the child strives to model himself upon the parent in a day-to-day association.

The Greek sense of disciple further implies that one undergoes systematic practices with the guidance of the master who is accomplished in them. Apprenticing a student does not mean conveying information. It is not an intellectual endeavor. The disciple is one who is trained, not informed. There is a regimen implied in the meaning of apprenticeship.

Interestingly, the New Testament uses the word apprentice without once designating the skill involved. When the word is used without a referent, then the tacit implication allows for a specific interpretation in the Greek speaking Jewish culture. The apprenticeship focuses upon the acquisition of the holiness and wisdom of the Torah. Quite emphatically, Jesus asserts his role in regard to the Torah: "Do not imagine that I have come to abolish the Torah or the Prophets. I have come not to abolish but to complete . . ." (Matthew 5:17) Into that completion he draws his disciples.

Torah is often translated as Law. The English speaking reader obviously invests the word "law" with juridical overtones. The Torah, however, has no connection with a formal piety governed by law. Torah means knowing the divine ways so that one becomes transformed by them. To know the Torah is an existential knowledge that touches the whole person. Learning the Torah had little to do with memorizing the words of Moses and the prophets. Matthew's entire Gospel emphasizes that Jesus identified his mission with the implementation of the Torah. As a Master of the Torah, his business was to demonstrate how one could attain the purpose of the Torah, namely, to become as perfect as one's heavenly Father (Matthew 5:48). More than intellectual familiarity or compliance with liturgical rites, the learning of the Torah required a personal transformation.

In his role as Master of the Torah, Jesus is referred to in the Gospels as "Master" (*didaskelos*) 45 times. Insufficient attention has been noted in the Gospel texts that record "master" as the most frequent title given to him. The texts indicate that he was involved in the preparation of a group of people who would assist him with his mission. This preparation is best understood by readers today in recalling the Eastern mentality in its understanding of the master-disciple apprenticeship. This model, as we will see, brings out meanings that conventional theology overlooks in Jesus' relationship with his selected group.

To aid the reader further in showing the importance of the word "master", let us contrast it with the designation of Jesus as "prophet". The word "prophet" (*propetes*) is applied to Jesus only 13 times in the Gospels. From a study of the Gospel stories, Jesus does engage in prophetic utterances. Yet the citing of him as "master" occurs with such frequency that the New Testament writers leave no doubt about which functional role assumed emphasis. In the Jewish culture the prophet publicly announced religious news that affected the community's spiritual survival. He spoke to the crowds, seeking to deliver a message in an oratorical style that moved the people to consideration. His urgent appeal was not in the interest of attracting followers, but rather in the interest of jarring minds to change the direction of their lives.

The master's approach was entirely different. He gathered a select group. His instructions were not so much in delivering a timely message as in instilling ways for his trainees to alter their understanding of reality. The prophet's concern for his audience is to arouse them, to take his message to heart. He is not interested in acquiring disciples. The master likewise concerns himself with the state of mind and lifestyle of his disciples, but with an intensity and intimacy that is reserved exclusively for them. Jesus enacted both roles, speaking to the public as a prophet, and to his disciples as a master.

The Significance of Sitting
The Gospels narrate:

> Seeing the crowds, he went up the mountain. There he sat down and was joined by his disciples. Opening his mouth, he apprenticed them . . . (Matthew 5:1–2)

Daily in the temple courtyard, I sat apprenticing. . . .
(Matthew 26:55)

The posture of sitting is a traditional one found in the East.
One could officiate at a synagogue or lecture to crowds from a
standing position. Sitting, however, was a sign of a special
activity. To sit meant that the master was ready to apprentice
his students. Swami Rama of the Himalayas, who was trained
in the traditional master–disciple association, has mentioned that
a genuine teacher should be able to sit quietly for a very long
time. Moreover, a teacher will not teach someone who fidgets
and constantly alters his posture. The quieting of the body
means that there is an internal calmness of mind disposed now
to listen and absorb the teachings.

In the most ancient spiritual tradition of the Himalayas, sitting
near a master in this manner is called, in Sanskrit, upanishad.
The recorded oral transmission (*smrti*) of the ancient sittings
were collected under the title *Upanishads*. These writings were
the vedanta, the cream of the *Vedas*. They summarized the
realized wisdom of the vedic seers. The masters would initiate
their chosen students or *chelas* into the ways in which the trainee
would personally arrive at the same universal insight. Teaching
the upanishad meant an apprenticeship for the disciple who
embarked upon a strict training program. The goal of this
master–disciple apprenticeship was to bring the chela's level of
consciousness to the self-same awareness that the upanishadic
master possessed.

In the collection of upanishad scriptures, the reader can peruse
the stories and statements which distill the original state of
consciousness. The actual training methods, those psychosomatic exercises that eventually produce the conversion to a new
state of consciousness are excluded. These revered practices –
sadhana or *prayoga shastras* – are the essence of the apprenticeship.
These practices are deftly inculcated to the disciple when the

master views him as ready. Involved is a complex relationship that affects the entire lifestyle of the student.

The student's faith in the master is never passive. At first, the student may have reservations and doubts. But as he prepares himself by the daily assimilation of the prescribed practices, his confidence in them grows. He experiences the results in himself. With the disciple's progressive assimilation of the psycho-dynamic practices, the master can lead the student further. Unless the disciple practices there is obviously no assimilation; the master cannot lead him further. Advanced practices would be withheld since the integrated readiness is absent. Whence the Gospel admonishment: "Many are called but few are chosen." (Matthew 22:14).

The chosen ones qualify by their determined efforts. They have made themselves ready. The questionable believer now becomes the experienced disciple.

The upanishadic experience of sitting near the seer has been the model for the yoga master throughout the centuries. It is the accepted norm when a teacher desires to impart his universal wisdom. At times the conduct and words of the master seem rationally indefensible. The student goes through periods of doubt and suspicion, even resentment. The master constantly challenges the rigidity of outlook as when Jesus cautions James and John about being destructively competitive because someone outside the group was also getting equal results. Throughout all the vicissitudes of the apprenticeship, the master will advise the student: if the disciple is not benefitting, or if the master is selfish, then the student should quickly depart.

Contemporary Misreading of the Gospels

Our analysis of the master–disciple relationship shows that a direct English reading into the texts does not convey the proper meaning of these terms. The usual interpretation by sincere believers of the master–disciple passages carries the impression that Jesus was an instructor giving lessons in religious information. Among church denominations emphasizing biblical indoctrinations, Jesus is seen to have preached to believers. Then, to insure that the disciples got the message, God worked mysteriously in their minds the enlightenment necessary to accept Jesus' instructions. The disciples then received the faith which transformed their lives. This resembles a passive process in which the disciple's personal initiative counted little.

What is suggested by the textual elaboration of the master-disciple relationship is an entirely different perspective. Jesus initiated his chosen students into discipleship which altered their consciousness. They trained themselves under his guidance in performance skills that were to equal and exceed his own:

> He who believes in me will also do the works that I do and greater works than these will he do (John 14:12).

Modern Christians do not view themselves as trainees but as believers. They are followers of Jesus like the crowds mentioned in the scriptures. Jesus spoke to these people but he did not consider them his disciples. The crowds may have believed and hoped in the words of Jesus but they could not realize the achievement of the disciples without the necessary apprenticeship. The question that emerges today is: What has happened to the tradition of apprenticeship in the churches? Where does one find the performance skills demonstrated by the disciples in the Book of Acts?

Faith and Apprenticeship

If there is a single word that characterizes the disposition that Jesus' followers had towards him during his public life, it was "faith". The English language uses two words – faith and belief – for the original Greek meaning of the verb, *pisteuein*, which means "to believe". Thus one speaks of having faith or the act of believing. Scholars admit that the New Testament writers borrow the Greek meaning exactly. The various meanings that faith possesses in the minds of contemporary Christians is more a denominational preference than an analysis of the Greek sense of the word.

Placing faith within the context of apprenticeship underscores a meaning of faith that is not obvious in the churches today. Faith in its Greek usage conveyed the meaning "to trust", "to rely on." In this sense of the word, a disciple's entrance into the apprentice relationship would require faith. In listening to a speaker or coming into the presence of a dynamic teacher, one can feel the attraction toward the person. The speaker's presence and his message can draw to himself an angry or an admiring crowd. Individuals may want to pursue further their spontaneous acceptance of this personage. All the reasons for the attraction may not be rationally evident until later reflection. Somehow, though, the listener was touched by the experience. This positive disposition to trust in the speaker is faith for the Greeks.

Belief, then, is quite an ordinary response in daily life; one accepts another person for himself and for what he stands. The more exposure to a person, the more one's trust or mistrust grows. In this way credibility becomes established or abolished. It can apply similarly to trusting or having faith in oneself.

The initial phase of an apprenticeship could very well be either infatuation or a certain ambivalence. One could be emotionally thrilled by the teacher's message and thus believe uncritically, or one could be intrigued and yet have reservations. Either response would be understandable.

When Jesus announced his vision of life, there is recorded in the scriptures a whole spectrum of responses. Some felt hostility, others were awed. A few decided to entrust themselves for awhile and become apprenticed to him: "Immediately they left their nets and followed him" (Matthew 4:20)

The act of faith is the ordinary human initiative to trust another person. Faith is one's choice. As the relationship develops, there will no doubt be opportunity for correcting earlier presuppositions. In the Eastern tradition of *gurudev-chela*, (master-student), the master is very much aware of his student's struggle with faith. The master carefully guides him through life experiences that challenge his current limitations in life. These life experiences become the vehicle for learning about imposed restrictions, thus expanding consciousness. Clarification is not always sweet and easy. Nevertheless, the disciple must struggle with his understanding of reality in order to fathom the master's teachings. Without inner struggle, faith remains vague and imaginary.

Faith in the master, however, amounts to more than an abstract credal statement. The circumstances of the master-disciple interplay involve a series of trying experiences for the aspirant. The cunning master knows with clarity the specific ingredients necessary for his student's spiritual improvement. The disciple fails, at times, to comprehend the master's deeds and words. Insight comes hard. Obstacles are self-imposed.

The master often appears unorthodox. His ways sometimes baffle, since the disciple is so limited in his conception of spiritual growth. The master's purpose is not to check the disciple's enthusiasm, but to encourage him to follow out the implications of the practices. The disciple's improved understanding of the lessons of life follows upon his personal practices. These spiritual exercises produce in the practitioner the dynamic alteration that enables a new vision of life. In their use, these exercises stimulate the practitioner's capacity for self-knowlege, bringing about drastic changes. Practice affects vision. The disciples of Jesus, for example, were taught how to use their inner energy for the plight of the ill and crippled. Through the experience of this dynamic ability, the disciples would not only realize anew their own worth, but appreciate the value of their master. It is in this marvelous display of their independent powers that the disciples are enabled to estimate how far they have come in their apprenticeship and appreciate its worth.

On occasions when the master would demonstrate his wondrous healing powers to the disciples, they would naturally be more in awe than comprehension. Later, after being trained in the augmenting and use of this inner power, they would realize that they too shared in the same life force.

Contemporary theology places the miraculous events narrated in the Gospels beyond the pale of ordinary believers. In a sense, this is true. Most believers, then as now, would not have undergone the necessary training to prepare themselves for expressing the inner power. Being unfamiliar with the possibility and nature of this human power, believers view it as exceeding their competence. In other words, they have no faith in themselves. This kind of deficiency reflects in the puzzled reactions narrated in the Gospels about Jesus' identity. The problem is not with the master's proficient and discreet exposure of his power. The problem is with the believer's lack of faith in himself. As long as the disciple has self-doubts, these weaknesses restrict his understanding of the master's identity. Without self-trust, without relying upon the human power within himself, the disciple remains constrained by his suspicions and weak in his resolve. Thus, the master remains an enigma: Who do men say I am? (Matthew 16:13).

Faith by itself does not transform. Faith fosters the mental attitude and emotional readiness not to limit the power of human consciousness. The disciple says, in effect, "I will believe, train, and see what happens." Faith is like a hypothesis. Although all the proof is not available yet, one goes about life as though the thesis is self-evident. It is the master's business to challenge any cultural restriction within the disciple's mind that restrains his potential growth. Through words and deeds and especially through silence, the master coaxes, pressures, stimulates, even commands the disciple to continue practicing until the hypothesis is proven through experience.

The Disciples' Failure

The disciple's association with his master will have human feelings about it that need correction. Students often fantasize about their spiritual progress and the power of their master. Infatuation leads to exaggeration. Having made the mistakes himself, the master knows how difficult it is to stay grounded in reality. Consequently, he will not be averse to selecting harsh measures to bring his students back to the facts of life. Apprenticeship is not easy; it is strenuous and prolonged. There are moments of disillusionment. The master does not necessarily fulfill the student's expectations.

Revering the master is not enough. Having faith in the master is an elementary beginning. Fervent admiration may provoke interest but it will not effect transformation. The master does not need praise. He desires his disciples' actualization of their inherent capacities. The master assists the process; he is not a substitute for it. The work of apprenticeship is, above all else, the disciple's efforts that lead to new self-discovery.

An illustration of this principle of self-training occurs dramatically in the Gospel. Having performed successfully in the art of healing, the disciples take on a new challenge and utterly fail. They are obviously chagrined at this embarrassing situation. Matthew's acccount of their failed attempt to cast out a demonic influence from a boy (Matthew 17:14–20) becomes, for Jesus the master, the occasion for teaching a profound lesson.

The boy's father, still seeking a cure, implores Jesus to rectify the lad's disturbance. He relates also how the healers (disciples) failed to do the job. In response, Jesus stuns everyone involved: "Faithless and perverse generation! How much longer must I put up with you?" (Matthew 17:17). In spite of his rebuke, he cures the boy. No explanation is given for his exclamation. Instead, the Gospel narrator depicts a later scene where the disciples are apparently alone with Jesus and they press him: "Why were we unable to expel it?" (Matthew 17:20).

Let us interject here. If these disciples understood healing the way modern Christians do, then they should have revised the question along these lines: "Why did not God work through us to heal the boy?" or "Why did not you, our master, extend your divine power through us as your instruments and thus effect a cure?" There is no hint at this interpretation. On the contrary, the disciples expected to cure the boy. They were experienced in healing. It was not their first attempt. Did Jesus hold back some technique required in this instance? Did the disciples, as it were, run out of healing power? Did God ordain to hold his grace of healing from the disciples' efforts? Speculation could wander in many directions.

Jesus' reply to their consternation is almost too simple. The disciples failed because they had too "little faith." Then Jesus makes his point with his faulty students: "If your faith were the size of a mustard seed, you could say to this mountain, 'move from here to here,' and it would move; for nothing would be impossible to you" (Matthew 17:21).

The striking use of the metaphor, mountain, would remind the disciples of their prodigious potential. Physically moving a mountain seems absurd. Yet if the disciples could overcome their lack of faith, even a mountain could not resist them. The question of weak faith pertains to themselves. Jesus does not remind his disciples that they should pray next time and then God will work his healing miracle through their humble submission. In fact, earlier he advised them not to multiply prayers (Matthew 6:7) and not to pray in public (Matthew 6:5). Jesus does not hint at their lack of faith in himself or in God; the issue is their lack of faith in themselves.

Their question was not why did God fail but why did "we" fail. Jesus is not trying to instruct them in the idea that they are nothing and God does it all. The disciple's failure to procure the anticipated healing is a failure of nerve. Jesus bluntly tells them they do not have enough trust in themselves. He reminds them that they, not God, are to move mountains.

Jesus' sarcasm is consistent with the master-disciple model.

The master's responsibility is not to pick up the pieces of his student's failures, but to induce in them the strength of self-confidence. If they do not build their self-trust, then their inherent powers remain dormant. His scolding reminds them just who is responsible.

Insisting in this way on the disciples' need for more self-determination does not detract from their acknowledgement of the Jewish God. Showing pious deference to God is not the issue. These students are being trained to discover and use their powers properly. Substituting God's agency in the face of a challenge to these powers dodges the purpose of their training.

Once the reader recognizes the consistent use of this master model in the Gospels for designating Jesus' most frequent activity, then many other biblical passages become clarified. To the crowds, Jesus preached; to his disciples, he taught through the mode of apprenticeship. Unfortunately we are only given some of the highlights of their resultant practices and not the specific exercises that account for their achievements. Nowhere do the listed Gospels narrate, for example, the specific techniques for healing. This reluctance of the Gospel writers is also quite customary. Operational techniques are seldom revealed in writing. They are individually handed on to the prepared disciple, lest they be abused or trivialized in a public exposition. In the East, masters appraise their spiritual knowledge as a sacred trust.

The lingering question is, What has happened to that trust since the Apostolic era? The master-disciple pattern of spiritual development has always been a personalized process whereby the disciple matures into a master himself. Then he passes on the spiritual tradition to his disciples. As Christianity developed after the first generation disciples, a double trend occurred. The new converts were initiated — baptized — into the mysteries of Christianity and given their instructions and offices of responsibility. The Christian religion became slowly institutionalized with all the advantages and disadvantages that accompany institutionalization.

In addition, the first two hundred years of Christianity showed an amazing diversity of emphasis and interpretation among the "followers of the way" as the Christians were then called. Already one finds a diverse emphasis mentioned in the Acts between Peter and Paul.

Among this spectrum of Christian followers was a thrust to continue a more meditative form of living. Groups of men and women formed communities, usually in the villages and rural areas rather than in the cities. Many individuals preferred to live more solitary lives and became mountain hermits. Historians have designated this tradition as the lives of the Desert Fathers. It was in this type of environment that the master-disciple association was preserved. Over the centuries this tradition likewise became structured and formalized into monasteries and convents in keeping with the vast organizational trend of Christianity. As Western culture and Christendom continued to interact over the years, the master-disciple pattern underwent changes. The clergy now assumed by their office as ordained ministers the rights and duties of spiritual guides. Occasionally, the emergence of a saint in society would attract a cult following and people would be inspired to pattern their lives after this individual's example and words.

The monastic atmosphere and the growth of seminaries in modern times developed a type of preparation to meet the needs of the Church in its confrontation with modern society. The older master-disciple pattern receded into forgotten memory. Officially, it was no longer endorsed. Modern times saw all the various denominations stress the need for devotional prayer and attendance at community services. Roman Catholicism emphasized the sacraments as the principal means for spiritual growth since this approach was under the regulation of the clergy. Even in monasteries and convents where there was still some echo of the older master-disciple association, it was still secondary to the formal sacramental activity of the monks and nuns. The protestant churches, in their various ways, emphasized individual interpretation of the Bible and private acceptance of Jesus Christ as Saviour.

There is still one area of Christianity, however, that reveres the older tradition of the master-disciple association. The orthodox monasteries on the penninsula of Mount Athos preserve the tradition of the Desert Fathers. These monasteries on the extremely rugged mountain peninsula of Greece have arranged their monastic lifestyles to draw upon the texts and techniques from the original texts of the first hermits along with the writings of those saints produced through the centuries. For those who have prepared themselves, cave life is also available.

While entrance into this ascetic lifestyle is restricted to celibate monks, there is today a definite but uneven return to the Gospel pattern of master and disciple for a growing number of Christians. Due to the influence of writers like Thomas Merton, William Johnston and Bede Griffith, Christians are becoming reacquainted with the enlivening power of the meditative traditions. Nuns and ministers have joined the laity in entering into Eastern monasteries as disciples to learn yoga and zazen techniques of meditation from acknowledged masters. Some newer monastic foundations are deliberately structuring their mode of spiritual living along the lines of Eastern *ashrams* and *zendos*.

These voluntary experiments in self-knowledge are answering an increasing desire in Christians to broaden their personal responsibility in their spiritual quest. If this healthy trend continues, then the twenty-first century may well see seekers transformed into saints and erudition into enlightenment.

CHAPTER 10

Miracles, Siddhis and Science

During World War I some Arab tribes were exposed for the first time to the telegraph. They considered the event divinely miraculous, until someone taught them how to operate the device. Some years later, in an obscure village tucked away in the Italian Alps, a citizen returning from a trip to Rome informed the villagers that the United States had just placed the first man on the moon. Awestruck, the people quickly crossed themselves and declared a miracle. Everyone knew that man had no such power; only God ruled the heavens.

In their non-technological worldview, both the Semitic tribe as well as the Italian villagers found it difficult to believe that man could naturally fulfill these announcements. The presence of an electronic apparatus for the Arabs and the story of space travel for the Italians could not help but produce astonishment – which is the proper incentive for declaring miracles. Alas, when knowledge dawned, the miraculous vanished. For our villagers, knowledge and miracle offset one another.

Before explaining the yogic view of miracles, let us first review the contemporary understanding of miracles for Christians. The Christian tradition of the miraculous traces its origins to the miracles of Jesus and his disciples in the New Testament. Throughout the development of Christianity, however, various religious leaders have interpreted the tradition differently. Let us, for instance, reach back into the stirrings of Protestant Christianity for its explanation of miracles.

In his *Sermons on St John*, Martin Luther mentions that the:

Apostles have preached the word and have given their writings, and nothing more than what they have written remains to be revealed, no new and special revelation or miracle is necessary.[1]

Luther's reading of scriptures led him to conclude that the days of the Christian miracle-working ceased with the death of the Apostles. People of his time needed only to hear the word of the Lord, rather than witness wonders. Luther reminds us of the Pauline injunction that faith is acquired through hearing the word. Therefore converting men spiritually through the office of preaching was, for Luther, an immeasurably greater task than miracle working.

Another dominant influence in Protestantism, John Calvin, insisted that after the Apostles, Christians were no longer permitted the power of miracles. He states in his *Institutes* that:

The gift of healing disappeared with the other miraculous powers which the Lord was pleased to give for a time, that it might render the new preaching of the gospel for ever wonderful.[2]

A similar judgment upon miracles is echoed in contemporary theology by some of the most influential churchmen. Karl Barth's writings acknowledge the presence of miracles at the Apostolic period but see no reason for God's power to enter into our world again on such a scale.[3] He insisted that God's holy spirit functions today only to dispose men's minds to accept in faith the biblical episodes. This view is seconded by such notable theologians as Dietrich Bonhoeffer, Paul Tillich and Bishop John A. T. Robinson.

But the contemporary school of thought that receives the largest following among scriptural scholars and churchmen today is Rudolph Bultmann:

> The whole conception of the world which is presupposed
> in the preaching of Jesus as in the New Testament generally
> is mythological, i.e., the conception of the world as being
> structured in three stories, heaven, earth, and hell; the
> conception of the intervention of supernatural powers in the
> course of events; and the conception of miracles, especially
> the conception of the intervention of supernatural powers in
> the inner life of the soul. . . . [4]

According to Bultmann, modern man, living in a scientific age,
must retain his critical sense in professing religion. The biblical
world and its descriptions of events has little in common with
our industrialized civilization. The modern believer must scale
down the biblical "myths" in order that the Gospel messages
have an acceptance in our nuclear age. The biblical passages
require what Bultmann calls "demythologizing": the miraculous
dimension as a factual account must be rejected. The miracles
did not happen. In reality, according to Bultmann, the faith of
the early Christians was conveyed in mythological descriptions
that appear to modern readers as concrete miraculous events.
Once we analyse the peculiarities of the biblical language and
the unscientific, primitive worldview possessed by the Gospel
writers, then we can understand the non-miraculous meaning
behind these faith-created stories. Bultmann thought that one
has to strip the mythological language away from the real event
that took place in order to avoid the modern 'superstitious'
evaluation that these events were miraculous.

Both Bultmann and Barth want to distinguish carefully two
separate spheres of existence. God's existence in his absolute
transcendence is opposite to man's in his frail, incomplete and
transitory material world. The opposition is total and complete.
The distance between man and God is an infinite abyss. Man's
nature is incapable of crossing it. By exaggerated confidence in
his own ingenuity, man only keeps himself from God. The only
way to cross the abyss, for Barth, is by man's return to biblical

faith. Humanity's world of arts and sciences cannot in any way enable man to reconcile himself to God. Man's hope in himself ends in chaos as seen in the event of World War I.

According to these theologians God is in heaven and man is on earth – two different beings, two different kingdoms. Man's natural powers of intellect and will, which have fashioned his flawed technocratic world, are absurdly useless in making any kind of contact with the divine kingdom. The condition of man's inability to communicate with God is theologically and religiously known as his fallen and sinful condition. The only solution to this dilemma is through God's condescension to humanity in the form of Jesus Christ, sent by the Father to redeem the situation. Man is saved from the confines of his defective nature and limited world through faith in Jesus, who by his perfect nature as the God-man breached the abyss. Christian faith in Jesus saves man from his tragic isolation on earth and provides meaning to human existence.

Barth views miracles as belonging to God's exclusive power. He affirms that these wondrous events manifested in man's world during the Apostolic period, but for him the attestation of miracles ceases there.

Bultmann equally emphasizes the role of faith in man's deliverance from his fallen condition. But he prefers a different evaluation for the Apostolic period which apparently recorded miraculous events. Some excerpts from his main essay, "Kerygma and Myth", establish his convergence on the problem of miracles:

> Man's knowledge and mastery of the world have advanced to such an extent through science and technology that it is no longer possible for anyone seriously to hold the New Testament view of the world . . . The miracles of the New Testament have ceased to be miraculous . . . It is impossible to use electric light and the wireless and to avail ourselves of modern medical and surgical discoveries, and at the same

time to believe in the New Testament world of spirits and miracles.[5]

For Bultmann, the danger of insisting upon these biblical 'myths' lies in presenting an unintelligible and unacceptable Christian faith to modern sophistication.

He sees our present day scientific understanding as one of the criteria with which to judge the early Apostolic writers. He does not think that these writers falsified their narrative, but rather that the imagery and figures of speech in the ancient Semitic-Roman world were the only tools available to be utilized by the faith interpretation of these Christian authors. Since modern understanding of energy and matter could not be available in their culture, how could they be held literally responsible for appealing to the modern mind? If modern science truly understands man and his world, then a Christian cannot be a fundamentalist about the Bible. Even more than Barth, Bultmann insists that no divine agency would interrupt the natural laws of our cosmos. The ignorance of the workings of nature in past cultures is continuously rectified by the advances of scientific progress.

From our overview of Western Christianity three basic theories regarding miracles can be seen.

1. *Apostolic Dispensation.* In this theory God allowed miracles in order to establish the credibility of the Christian church during the Apostolic period. These miracles reinforced Jesus' message. Once the Church was secure in the Mediterranean area, God withdrew his dispensation.

2. *Mythological.* In this theory the miracles did not happen in a concrete, literal manner. The miracle passages of the Bible are not factual accounts but symbolic descriptions. When Jesus cured the blind man, for example, this incident should be read as spiritual blindness; the raising of the dead points out that one who is dead in spirit may recover religious life anew. This

theory depicts the miracle stories as allegorical descriptions. Theories 1 and 2 are held by most mainline Protestant churches.

3. *Divine Intervention.* In this theory the biblical passages are accurate accounts. Yet throughout history, as witnessed by saintly people and special places (Lourdes, Fatima, other shrines, articles and relics of saints), God has intervened and permitted a dispensation of his power beyond the apostolic period for special people and occasions. This view is generally held by Roman Catholic churchmen.

While most modern theologians of mainline denominations would concur with the above threefold division, there are, nonetheless, Christian groups who have considered miracles as a normal functioning of their evangelizing. The Pentecostal, Fundamentalist and Christian Science Churches, for example, have always recognized and even encouraged the divine phenomenon of "healing" miracles. Currently, there is also the trend known among many different denominations as the Charismatic movement. Among these believers, the power of the Christian God, in some mysterious manner, may affect relief or a cure for an ill person. Usually, these positive results require the instrumental aid of the official minister or designated healer within the group. But any authentic miracles of healing are attributed solely to divine agency. The divine intervention persists in history and, on the basis of its scriptural interpretation, may be called down upon the Christian community.

Miracles in the New Testament

A miracle in the traditional sense certainly isn't an ordinary occurrence in our times. For Saint Augustine a miracle meant:

> something difficult, which seldom occurs, surpassing the faculty of nature and going far beyond our hopes as to compel our astonishment.[6]

Derived from Latin, the word means "something admirable",

or "extraordinarily wonderful", an event that would not be unnatural but exceeding the normal laws of time, space, and causality. In Acts it is recorded:

> The many signs and wonders worked through the Apostles made an awesome impression on everyone (Acts 2:45).

> Many signs and wonders were worked among the people by the hands of the Apostles (Act 5:12).

Throughout the scriptures there are numerous passages describing awesome signs such as healings, prophecy, resuscitation to life, clairvoyance, transmutation of matter, levitation, and others. Actually, the biblical text uses three words for miracles: *dunamis, semeion* and *teras*. These Greek words may be translated respectively as "dynamic power," "signs or significant acts," and "a marvel or something that stirs excitement". The latter meaning always appears in the text with *semeion*, as in signs and wonders. Paul writes:

> You have seen done among you all the things that mark the true apostle, unfailingly produced: the signs, the marvels, the miracles (Cor 12:12).

The thirteenth Apostle is merely calling attention to what Jesus had already counseled his disciples about – their duplicating his wondrous deeds, even surpassing the Son of Man. The Bible, of course, does not narrate the entire careers of the disciples, let alone of Jesus. There is, no doubt, a connection between the performance of miracles and association with Jesus in some way, for the more these disciples pursued their relationship with Jesus, the more they manifested similar powers over nature.

The Relationship between Body, Mind and Nature

The biblical accounts of this disciple relationship and the connection to miraculous powers are paralleled in the yoga tradition, which at this point can shed light on their explanation.

Human consciousness has the inner capacity to observe its functionings at work. By a simple inner reflection, one can watch his own interior mental operations. From fragmentary ideas and impressions to complex concepts, one can witness his mind endlessly absorbing and shaping its mental interior. In yoga psychology the mind-stuff which undergoes continual modifications is called *chitta*. When this mind-stuff assumes a shape (*chitta* taking form), then the modification of *chitta* is called a *vritti*. Human maturity is measured by the increased ability to assume control over the mental faculties and their expressions.[7]

Strange as it may seem, yoga philosophy considers the mind and all its fluctuations as belonging to the realm of material being. Thinking, judging, desiring or remembering – even the slightest fluctuation or mental act – are considered vibrations of matter. Thus, mind as well as body remains subject to the natural laws of material being. Certainly the body differs from the mind, but this distinction is only relative, for there exists an organic communion between them. Mind and body together share existence at the level of nature. Both are possessed by and subject to the field of material being. Yoga refers to this universal field of matter as *prakrti*.

Nature does not resist man's effort to know it. On the contrary, nature, or *prakrti* (the world of matter), has an affinity towards man's act of awareness; otherwise, the world would not be knowable. Energy, in other words, is at the service of consciousness.[8]

The conscious life center in man is called the *purusha*, the innermost knowing self, being akin to the Christian notion of soul as a life principle.[9] By invoking the law of self-concentration, one can extend his mind's influence over the body. One notices that exercising the body with attention produces agility.

The awkwardness between mind and body smooths out. Increasing the awareness of the body makes the body more amenable to the mind's intention.

The art of awareness whereby both the mind and the body are brought under self-control is called meditation. The practice of meditation can extend mental control to encompass the mind and body's subtle areas including the autonomic nervous system and the entire subconscious.[10]

When the yogi improves his meditation by developing a one-pointedness or *samyama* upon some aspect of matter, the focal point of interest comes under full control.[11] The entire intelligibility of the object of concentration is within his grasp. Comprehending something in this manner is not an intellectual exercise like learning the rudiments of geometry or how to diagram a compound sentence. Hardly. In focusing its penetrative power, consciousness apprehends not only the obvious sensual and intellectual arrangements of an object, the cognitive aspects available to rational knowing, but the entire range of its potentialities, including its history and destiny. *Samyama* means the mind assimilates an exhaustive inventory. All the knowable potentials, actual or latent, of nature can be thoroughly comprehended.

The laws of meditation expand consciousness, as it were, to cover or pervade *prakrti* at will. Intuition and control go together; to know is to control from within. The mind does not impose its dominance from the outside, the way one's hand moves the steering wheel of an auto. Rather, the dexterity any healthy person displays with his limbs, the yogi can perform with all bodies of matter.

Perfect intuition yields perfect control. Through his liberating practices of self-control, the accomplished yogi can consciously identify with matter freely, as though it were part of himself, and thus manipulate it.

Before gaining the ability to control nature, however, the yogi must acquire control over his individual *prakrti*. His bodily nature incessantly makes demands upon his person. Unless the resonance of these appetites is understood and trained, one remains at the whim of their unpredictable reactions.

Up to this point the disturbing features of *prakrti* produced by his agitated mind and body have prevented the yogi from realizing comprehensive awareness. The physical conditions of ill health, improper diet, an imbalanced lifestyle, anxieties, and similar problems prevent the necessary interior pacification demanded for awareness to reach its intuitional levels. Unless the adept properly trains himself in relation to his own *prakrti*, nature keeps her secrets hidden.

A certain pacification through meditation is the key. When the mind–body ensemble is calmed, a spontaneous unity emerges that gradually allows more and better control over bodily *prakrti*. The self or spirit slowly recovers a conscious autonomy over its resident matter. The spirit loosens its bonds with *prakrti*. By developing a tranquil integration of body, emotions and thought processes, the natural correlation between spirit and matter occurs. The bodily impulses, the emotional flarings, the dissipation of the nervous system, all recede into a calmness that frees the mind from preoccupation with these lesser aspects of human nature. No longer restricted to their demands but fully respecting them when need be, the adept heightens his awareness to more subtle ranges of energy within and without. Nature has been the object of his rational cognition; in addition, it now becomes the object of his intuitional awareness. In rational knowing, the object is only thought about from the outside; now the object is known from its inner essence. The object's past, present and future determinations are completely knowable and sublimated into the yogi's awareness.

Spiritual development always starts with the individual focusing upon his growth in self-understanding. When spiritual growth proceeds through tranquil self-control, nature or *prakrti* reveals itself as one substantial field capable of unlimited modifications. A person's individual mind and body are only relatively distinct energy configurations within this field. Reason, of course, in its discursive mode of apprehending the external world, certifies otherwise. It views the world as individual substances.

The yogi, however, from the superior vantage of meditative awareness, notices that every mental activity is an expression of *prakrti*. His apparent individuality is fundamentally a temporary differentiation of nature itself. Since his body and mind are a microcosm of the field of *prakrti*, they contain all the essential principles and factors found anywhere in nature. By deepening his interior calmness, the yogi gains a full intuition of the nature of *prakrti*. Already liberated from the disturbances of his body, mind and external circumstances, the yogi now converts his awareness into perfect control of *prakrti* in all its aspects. Having purified himself from egotism and other bondages, he is spiritually seasoned and prepared to accept responsibility for the secrets of the cosmos. Nature will now acquiesce to his will. The realm of the miraculous is now available to him.

The Yoga Account of Miracles

In the language of yoga, miracles are known as *siddhis*. The ancient scriptures called the *Yoga Sutras* describe in chapter three many of the various feats that Christian theologians would classify as miraculous. The Sutra texts include methods for achieving clairvoyance, healing power, invisibility, reading minds, bilocation, multiplying food, levitation and other phenomena that parallel the wonders of the New Testament. These abilities emerge as part of the natural development of spirituality.

In examining the biblical accounts of miraculous events with an understanding of the relationship between consciousness and *prakrti*, the performance of a miracle, or the demonstration of a *siddhi*, corresponds proportionally to the state of spiritual integrity. In this way, universal laws of spiritual development

provide for protection against their abuse. Before one can manifest truly supernatural or miraculous powers, there are certain
personal requirements demanded of the individual. Usually
these qualifications are prompted and groomed by a disciple
under the tutelage of someone already spiritually advanced. The
disciple-teacher relationship described in the Gospels is not
unique to the Semitic world, but is indigenous to the East. Once
a reader is familiar with this common spiritual training method,
then these Gospel stories easily fit into place.

The progress of the disciple is closely observed by his teacher
since the latter takes upon himself a lifelong responsibility to
assist his beloved students to their ultimate destiny. In their
progress toward spiritual integration, the students' self-understanding grows and the abilities known as miraculous powers
quite unassumingly emerge. Certain specific practices may be
involved which can accelerate or refine these emerging
capacities.

In rare instances some lesser powers (which are called psychic
abilities) may suddenly manifest from the subconscious without
the prescribed spiritual development. These instances may be
detrimental to the true spiritual seeker. Others, however,
misunderstand these occurrences in themselves and promote
their own vanity and financial possibilities, thus turning a
natural power into a spiritual deficit.

When ethical and psychological maturity is present in the
disciple, the performance of these miracles or *siddhis* is not
undertaken for self-aggrandizement. An examination of Jesus'
performance reveals a serious attitude in every one of his
miracles. There is never any effort to "show off" or tease the
crowd into admiring him. The absence of egotistical motiv-
ations is apparent, and from a close analysis of the character of
Jesus and other great sages one can obtain insight into the
personal characteristics demanded of those who would call upon
nature to obey them.

It may come more as a shock than a surprise for many Christians to learn that for centuries, even before Jesus' time, the performance of miraculous events has been a natural expression of a yogi's development. This is not to say that yogis occupy their time displaying miraculous powers. They are as discriminating as Jesus was in using his powers. There is abundant evidence that Jesus' miracles have been duplicated by yogis as well as other spiritual traditions throughout the world. The Old Testament likewise records similar miraculous events as found among Jesus and his disciples.

It is not difficult to compare a list of Gospel miracles with the recorded *siddhis* of revered yogis. In this century alone, the lives of Rama Tirtha, Aurobindo, Anandamayi Ma, Ramana Maharishi and others demonstrate the same miraculous performances as narrated in the New Testament.

Anandamayi Ma, an Indian saint who left her body in 1982, showed her compassion toward those afflicted by healing them with a word or a touch. One episode is related in which one of her students was suffering from a severe crippling of the spine. When the student related his plight, Ma simply passed her hand over his spine and the pain vanished permanently. Another incident reminds one of Jesus' transfiguration. Ma began meditating with a group and announced that they should keep their eyes closed. Later, when they opened their eyes, they found a man lying unconscious in the hallway. Revived, he related that he came late and peeped into the room. He saw such an intense light radiating from Ma's face that he was unable to look at it and lost consciousness due to the overwhelming energy.[12]

Neem Karoli Baba, a yogi of northern India, had the *siddhi* of Annapurna and was able to multiply food for his devotees as Christ did for the multitudes. An unusual intervention occurred when a student remarked how it was impossible for him to become a physician since he was a second-rate student and could not gain admittance to medical school. Baba simply touched the young man's head. Shortly thereafter the man was admitted to medical school and distinguished himself academically.[13]

Sri Swami Rama of the Himalayas tells the story of how he and his master were traversing a steep mountain path when an avalanche started towards them. Being in its direct path they seemed doomed. The master just raised his hand, stopping the avalanche in mid air. When they reached the other side of the path, he waved his hand and the avalanche continued down the mountain side.[14]

There are countless other stories about yogis and saints that exactly resemble the episodes in the Gospels. The yogi views the miracle or *siddhi* as the natural outcome of certain spiritual development. In fact, many of these *siddhis* come early in the path of spirituality before the aspirant has refined himself into a saint. The miraculous is not a power bestowed upon someone by an external agent – God or otherwise – but a natural unfoldment of latent abilities within human consciousness. These inherent powers are therefore not properly understood by evaluating them as performances of a divine agent intervening with natural laws.

Until modern science attained acceptance as a contributing factor in Western society, people often attributed the causal explanations for natural phenomena to divine intervention. Hence superstition abounded in the European mind. It took centuries before people realized that attributing the causal factors of natural events to God's intervening action does not truly explain the facts. The strong religious faith of the Middle Ages and the post-reformational centuries plus the limited understanding of the laws of nature combined to produce a static religious interpretaton of the world, which for the most part, endorsed God rather than alternative, natural explanations. Even penalties were affixed to unorthodox theories. Whenever science touched upon an interpretation that was considered the domain of religion, such as in cosmological theories, the nature of man and his faculties, creation and evolution, to name but a few, censorial treatment often ensued.

Two tragic episodes involve the scientists Giordano Bruno,

who was burned at the stake by the ecclesiastical authorities, and Galilee Galileo, who was forced to recant his theories before the Christian inquisition and was placed under house arrest for the rest of his life. Throughout the centuries many of the theories of these men, and others like them, were accepted as orthodox science, due to the growing power and independence of scientific research. Surprisingly, it was not until 1984 that the Roman Church admitted its error with the Galileo case.

The search for truth about reality may seem disruptive of the established worldview, but sometimes the advance of truth cannot avoid exposing the incompleteness of the current state of affairs.

The climate is changing today. Science and religion mutually respect each other's realms and attempt to accommodate themselves to their own limitations. However, this separation of science and religion may be too severe. Some religious authorities feel that scientific propositions can aid us in our understanding of religious truths. Bultmann, for example, is correct in his insistence that miracles meet the criticism of scientific investigation. Unfortunately, he carries this norm too far by denying any scientific respectability to these phenomena. Because he is unfamiliar with the evidence that yoga research provides which illustrates that "miracles" are based on profoundly subtle but natural laws, he presumes that the Gospel accounts are not to be taken in any objective sense.

On the other hand, Barth, who respects the biblical text as well as the domain of science, is reluctant to dismiss the Gospel wonders as merely religious poetry. His insistence that the miraculous phenomena occurred only during the apostolic era reveals an ultraconservative judgement about modern man's possibilities for miracles, as well as a narrow understanding of natural laws.

Both Protestant scholars revere the Gospel accounts and want to interpret them for modern man in the twentieth century. Neither one, however, is able to render a satisfactory explanation for the presence of miracles in history, let alone the accumulating evidence today that demonstrates that man's abilities far exceed what theologians and scientists of the early part of this century thought possible.

Likewise, Roman Catholic theologians are aware of the research in biofeedback and parapsychology, but have neglected to incorporate these findings into their understanding of the range of human possibilities. They too assume a too diminutive view of man's nature. The scientific data in various institutes in North America and Europe which explore the nature of consciousness and its control over bodily functions and material energy are forcing new implications in the area of man's nature for both science and religion.[15] Barth, Bultmann, and other theologians remain too incomplete in their basic analysis of man and his faculties. These men share this limitation with all Christian churches. Confronted with the deficiencies and accomplishments of ordinary people, they allow this behavior to be their prototype of human nature. In contrast with the normal portrait of man, they juxtapose Jesus Christ. Although Jesus manifested the same basic nature as others of the human race, the quality of his human expression sets him apart radically. No one would doubt his human competence. But whether theologians are justified in maintaining that Jesus' level of humanness is inaccessible to the rest of humanity, thereby indicating some essentially different kind of living being, requires more evidence than is generally found in theological manuals or scriptures.

Biblical texts state explicitly, and on more than one occasion, that Jesus' followers would be able to duplicate his wondrous feats – even supersede them. The description of the book of Acts narrates the astonishment of the citizens at the wonders and powers demonstrated by the disciples. Barth is quite reasonable in supposing that these divine gifts were necessary in order for people to realize the caliber of the Christian way. The question here, then, is why Barth and so many biblical scholars suddenly halt at this point, declaring what amounts to a moratorium on miracles.

The uneven history of saints and mystics belies this hesitancy on the part of religious scholarship. Holy men and women have abundantly expressed similar gifts or spiritual accomplishments in their recorded careers. Before and after the apostolic period, within Christianized cultures and elsewhere, a brief survey of religions and non-Christian spiritualities would easily support the identical array of miracles or *siddhis* that only prejudice would attribute to one example of religion.

To pose a scientific spirituality would not endanger the authenticity of divine truths embodied in a religion. On the contrary, a dialogue between yoga, science, and organized religion would help clear the air of reactionary suspicions and provide the background for a deeper appreciation of the mystery of Christ as well as the inherent dignity of man.

CHAPTER 11

Christian Gnosticism and Yoga

Near the pharaonic tombs of the sixth dynasty, half-way up the Nile towards Cairo, a remarkable discovery took place in 1945. This incident was hardly known outside the Middle East since the rest of the world was busy celebrating the end of World War II.

Searching for fertilizer, a camel driver found a large jar, one meter high, hidden in a cave. Cracking the vessel open, he watched a bundle of papyrus texts spill to the ground. At this point, various versions of the discovery are told. One account relates how the peasant hid his find in a corner of his house and ran to inform the authorities only to find the treasure being used by his mother to start the evening fire at his return. Another version has him selling the cache for three Egyptian pounds to an antique dealer.

Veiled with obscurity, there now begins a long trail of intrigue and professional competition among archeologists, museums and translators that delayed the discovery from reaching the English speaking world for over thirty years. The earthen jar had yielded fifty-one various manuscripts, forty-one of which were completely unknown to the amazed scholars. Fragments of letters and receipts used to reinforce the bindings bore dates to 333 A.D. Here was the most extensive document-ation to date of the early Christian sect known as the Gnostics.

These writings are collectively known as the *Nag Hammadi Library*, borrowed from the name of the small town near the spot of discovery, or the *Chenobaskion Manuscripts*, from a Chris-tian monastery in the same neighborhood. More extensive than the Dead Sea Scrolls discovered in 1947, these writings shed a rich and surprising light upon one of the most controversial periods of early Christianity. While not receiving notoriety outside academic circles, the contents of the *Nag Hammadi Library* may surprise Christians who read them.

Most Christians take it for granted that the New Testament contains only four Gospels, some letters, and the Book of Revelations. Yet the *Nag Hammadi Library* reveals the Gospels of Mary, Thomas, Philip, Truth and The Egyptians. There are the additional Revelations of James, Paul, Adam and Peter. Since the compilation of any Gospel occurred over a period of many years, it is not unusual that there could be more than the conventional four of the New Testament. What is perhaps the most surprising is the addition of strange new texts: Thunder, the Perfect Mind; the Second Word of the Great Seth; The Testimony of Truth; and The Dialogue of the Redeemer, to name but a few.

From a careful analysis of the *Nag Hammadi Library*, three conclusions are drawn. First, while duplicating the Gospel stories, the newly discovered manuscripts expand further the life of Jesus and his followers, often leading the reader to interpretations different from those upheld by mainline Christian churches. Second, the *Nag Hammadi Library* shows that there are many spiritual traditions, from the Greek to the Oriental, comprising the essence of Gnosticism. The texts called Teaching of Truth of Zostrianos, the God of Truth, and The Song of the Pearl would indicate the Persian tradition associated with the religion of Zoroastrianism, for example. Third, the *Nag Hammadi Library* shows that there was an inter-relationship between Gnosis and conventional Christianity as well as their independence from each other. A Christianizing of Gnosis and a Gnosticizing of Christianity occurred. Even the Church Fathers, the more orthodox theologians of the early Church, spoke of their true gnosis over and against the Gnostics' versions.

It is important never to lose sight of the historical fact that the Gnostics were not alien to the Christians, viewing themselves as an opposing religious sect, but in reality were mostly Christians who upheld beliefs which they considered genuinely Christian. St Paul himself expounds many ideas that are compatible and apparently identical with the Gnostic interpretation of Jesus and the Church. It is evident that there are instances in his epistles when he opposed them, yet there are more instances when he is completely in accord with them. In his letter to the Ephesians, for example, Paul portrays Jesus as the cosmic man (Ephesians 1:10) which is a Gnostic concept. His notion that flesh and spirit are irreconcilable (Romans 8:5–10; 13:11–13), as well as the idea that the spiritual Christ is decisive and not the earthly one (II Corinthians 5:16) are likewise Gnostic ideas. One can only speculate to what extent Paul's decision to use Gnostic ideas and terms came from his spiritual experience or his strictly rational reflections in finding them appropriate. That he used them is clearly evident.

The Meaning of Gnosis

The Greek word *Gnostic* means "knowledge or understanding." Its use in designating those sects of Christians in the first to the fifth centuries carries the nuance of a special type of knowledge. Unlike faith or intellectual knowledge, gnosis meant an esoteric or intuitive understanding that is inaccessible to rational analysis. In this sense gnosis is more akin to the *para vidya* of the Upanishads, a higher knowledge available to the ordinary mind which the yogis seek in *samadhi*. This special knowledge revealed the ultimate meaning of life and the universe.

> If anyone has gnosis, he is a being who comes from above . . . He knows like someone who was drunk and has become sober from his drunkeness and, restored again to himself, has again set his own in order (Gospel of Truth).[1]

In fact, the Gnostics ridicule denominational faith. In their eyes faith has at best a provisional role and can never be the only way to salvation. It is too narrow a premise going nowhere, since it is empty of immediate effect. This unyielding stance conflicted with the bishops' emphasis on the exclusive role of faith. That the Gnostics resisted any authoritative clergy in their ranks did not help their relations with the Christian Church. The Gnostic heritage dwelled upon those religious themes that would occupy the minds of any Christian: God, the world and human nature. Yet there was no emphasis upon a normative theology, no rule of faith or insistence upon the importance of dogma. This de-emphasis upon strict credentials of faith would be consistent with a movement that concerned itself more with an interior realization of these ideas than outward conformity. From an investigation of the *Nag Hammadi Library* texts, the Gnostics allowed a very diversified presentation of what one may broadly refer to as the Gnostic theology. Apparently this toleration for varying viewpoints carried over in their communities where there was a wide range of conduct from the bizarrely ritualistic to the purely internalized ascetic.

Historically, the Gnostics never encouraged conformity. Their concepts of God, human nature and the universe were considered so radical by the more conventional Christians that a large number of theologians wrote against them. Men like Justin (165 A.D.), Irenaeus (180 A.D.), Tertullian (200 A.D.), Hyppolytus (225 A.D.), Clement (200 A.D.), and Origin (250 A.D.) tried to expose the intellectual and moral dangers in the Gnostic thought. These authors, it is to be remembered, wrote against the Gnostics in a siege mentality, as it were, struggling to combat ideas and practices that they thought would seriously endanger the salvation of souls. Valuable as their polemical writings are, it is not unlikely that many quotations from the Gnostics were pulled out of context and passionate accusations took the place of fair critical analysis.

These tensions are all the more interesting in that the Gnostics produced the first and largest theological literature among Christian writings. The intensity of the polemic was during the second and third centuries. Afterwards the movement ebbed, probably due to the consolidation of Christianity under Emperor Constantine in 313 A.D. and the persistent pressure banning Gnostic ideas and writings.

The Scope of Gnosis

The Gnostic texts reveal a rich heritage of contributory sources and original reflection. Indo-Persian, Jewish, Greek, Egyptian and Christian concepts fill out the mosaic of its teachings. If one can leave aside, for the moment, the judgment of the Catholic bishops and theologians that saw Gnostic Christians misled at best, and the progeny of Satan at worst, then the major features of these writings provoke new questions even for our present day.

From the material of the *Nag Hammadi Library*, one sees that several divergent versions of the same theme are found side by side. Apparently, the Gnostic communities appreciated the manifold ways that a text could be interpreted. This method of taking an ancient text and rendering different implications from it was not so much an instance of subjectivism as an illustration of the untold depth of a tradition that required a varied approach in order to extract the fullness of meaning.

This method of explication is found throughout the East. The *Yoga Sutras* and the *Bhagavad Gita*, for example, have had many commentaries written about them over the centuries. What makes the *Nag Hammadi Library* discovery so interesting to scholars and readers is that the divergent views are all assembled together. Again, it must not be overlooked that the four conventional Gospels of the New Testament are not four successive chapters composing a single description of Jesus and his period. On the contrary, these Gospels provide four distinct portraits, similar to each other and yet individually interpreted to depict meaning that the others may or may not evidence. The narration of Jesus' birth in Matthew is radically different from the account in Luke; at face value they seem contradictory to each other.

The Gnostic writings show an ability to express ideas in ever new ways, borrowing from older traditions at times, and reframing the older mythological material for their purposes. The essential features of the Gnostic myth are readily available throughout the divergent texts. It is to these fundamental conceptions that our essay pertains.

The Gnostic Cosmos

The description of the universe – the Gnostic cosmology – was not invented afresh. The Gnostic teachers inherited a worldview typical to both semite and Christian. It was the Ptolemaic world with the earth at the center surrounded by air and eight heavenly spheres. These spheres contain the seven planets and the fixed stars. Beyond or above this geocentric astronomy is the realm of the unknown God residing in the *pleroma* or graduated worlds of "fullness." These two realms – the eternal world of God the Father with the heavenly hierarchy and the vast created world – are irreconcilable. The planetary spheres enclose "demons" or "rulers" that can exert unruly influence upon men. The chief ruler is the Demiurgos, the creator god who produced the phenomenal realm. Together this god and the invisible demons constitute the kingdom of "fate" for man. The treacherous cosmos is variously referred to as darkness, deception and death. These cosmic powers dominate the human condition through the signs of the zodiac.

The tyranny of the stars is unique to the Gnostics. While the Asiatic and Greek cosmologies found fault with the world, none of them equated matter with evil as did the Gnostics. The yogis who recognize the Vedanta philosophy may agree with the Gnostics about the deficiency and illusion of the universe, but would hardly speak of it being incorrigibly hostile. For the Gnostics the entire manifested world offered not the slightest pause from the relentless kingdom of darkness.

How did the cosmos get this way? The Gospel of Philip states:

> The World came into being through a transgression. For he who created it wanted to create it imperishable and immortal. He failed and did not attain to his hope.[2]

The natural world is an alluring mistake. While there are differences over the number of hostile powers, the Gnostics hold that mankind is induced by sinister spirits of all types to forget his higher nature and be subject to their unholy ends.

The complexities of the cosmic schema differ in various texts but the essential negative stance is the same. No wonder then that the Neo–Platonists, the Roman Stoics and the Church Fathers line up vigorously against the Gnostics. For in the eyes of these opponents, the cosmos was essentially sound, ruled by a beneficent creator, inspiring man by its beauty and order to pursue its divine origin. Similarly, in the Vedas, there are innumerable endorsements of the glory of the universe. It is from this positive beauty that the yogis draw their inspiration for transcendence.

> Even as the radiance of the Sun enlightens all regions, above, below, and slantwise, so that only God, glorious and worthy of worship, rules over all his creation. (Mundaka Upanishad)[3]

Human Nature and Destiny

Just as the sensual body and rational mind have an affinity for the world and its enticing snares, so with everyone there is an inner person possessing an eternal spark of light, according to Gnostic belief. This light is divine, the very essence of man. St Paul mentions the same concept in his letter to the Roman community reminding his followers to "cast off the works of darkness and put on the armour of light" (Romans 13:12).

Gnostic anthropology portrays a threefold composition of human nature. There is the flesh, or body, the psychic, or mind, and the self, or soul. The personality of each person is determined by which of the three elements – body, mind or spirit – predominates. The man of flesh is a captive to the world of illusion and transience. Enslaved of the devil, his soul is blind and deaf even to the need for salvation. The body is described as a robe or coat covering the mental dimension, attracted to the mire of creation. Man's capitulation to the vagaries of matter only increases his forgetfulness of his original true nature. Men are at war with themselves and the evil spirits, feeling at times a longing for a higher life but immediately opposed by mundane desires and passions which direct their energies otherwise. The biblical symbol indicating this personality is Cain.

The personality of the psychic or mental individual shows itself by developing his rational capacities. He stands in the middle between the carnal and the spiritual. He must choose his destiny, either aspiring to Gnosis or perishing in sensual mortality.

The pneumatic personality, the man of spirit, is aware of his relationship to God. In fact, his gradual self-knowledge brings the insight that he is a divine person. The Gnostic readily endorsed the Psalm verse, "You are gods, all sons of the most high" (Psalms 82:6). The biblical type for this personality is Seth.

In recognizing a divine core within man, the Gnostics submitted a new metaphysical status in the order of existence: man is above the creator god, the Demiurgos. It is man's kinship with the unknown god, the Father/Mother god, which, once awakened, enables him to return to the real kingdom and renounce the worthless world as his destiny.

Few men, however, will achieve the spiritual status of the elect or perfect ones who allow the light within to burn brightly forever. The reason for the paucity of members has been foretold in Genesis. The Adam and Eve story in various manuscripts reveal man's descent into matter and the struggle that everyone goes through. This biblical story is the prototype for the human condition, showing the need for redemption.

The Notion of Salvation

Men need salvation from the world. Redemption, resurrection and gnosis are equivalently understood as salvation. Instead of considering resurrection as a corporeal reuniting of a body with the soul after death – the conventional Christian appraisal – the Gnostics offered a complex assessment. Resurrection combined first the inflaming of the soul's spark of light. This resuscitation came through the call of a redeemer and especially through self-knowledge. In this way the ignorance of forgetfulness is overcome. Secondly, the liberated spirit ascends to the heavenly kingdom, the *pleroma*.

In some texts this spiritual consummation takes place at physical death while others insist it must occur before death. In the flexible presentation of the texts, perhaps it would be better to posit resurrection on two levels: one, a self-transformation in consciousness wherein the individual's experience of gnosis is like a rebirth or resurrection. (The word resurrection in Greek conveys the notions of a re-awakening as well as a raising.) Two, a final release from the corporeal dimension signified by death's irretrievable separation of spirit from matter. Here one finds an inconsistency with the Gnostic stand on matter. Some of the texts allow for the existence of a new body after death; a spiritual flesh ensues that acts as a bearer of the spirit. Apparently the body was not as abhorrent as previously claimed.

At the same time, individual resurrection depicts a later total consummation of the universe at the end of time. All souls will be properly disposed. Some, the elite, will enjoy eternal beatitude; others, not so lucky, will face eternal perdition. A world cyclic process is absent from the texts, for the cosmos will meet a final dissolution. In the meantime, the psychic or mental personalities will undergo reincarnation for a few times in hope that they will finally choose gnosis.

Dualism and the Role of a Redeemer

Gnosis embraces a dualism, metaphysical in scope, which divides the unknown god and the inner man on one side away from the creator-ruler god with his demonic army and the material universe. Being matter and spirit, man is a microcosm reflecting in himself the vast struggle between ignorance and knowledge, evil and good, perdition and enlightenment. The removal of ignorance, the barrier to salvation, is the process of gnosis. The Gospel of Philip states:

> Ignorance is a slave. Knowledge is freedom. When we recognize the truth we shall find the fruits of the truth in us. If we unite with it, it will bring our fulfillment.[4]

Unlike the comprehensive approach of yoga, Gnosticism has no insistence of an integration of body, mind and spirit for genuine freedom. Yet the gnostics do not posit liberation as an automatic event with no preparation. In many texts there is an emphasis upon ethical behavior and ascetical practices to reinforce and preserve the elite state. Gnostic liberation is basically self-redemption. The idea of a redeemer corresponds more to the role of an inspiring paradigm, someone who has demonstrated the possibility of freedom from the cosmos. This is quite similar to the role of *avatars* in Eastern thought.

The Gnostic texts, as expected, do not present a uniform necessity for a redeemer. For some, the redeemer is an emissary of light shining forth in the earthly darkness, a beacon of truth that illuminates the way. For others, the figure of Jesus has been mythologized into a central role. While the exclusive reliance upon redemption through a redeemer, as in orthodox circles, is foreign to the Gnostic mind, the representation of Jesus Christ at times assumes a special status. Jesus is the revealer and prophet of Gnostic wisdom. In the form of secret traditions, Jesus imparts this wisdom to his elect, often through the mediation of privileged disciples, such as Peter, James, John and Thomas. He is the light-person, the personification of God. His incarnation into time and space entails him to enter hell and confront the psychic demons that pervade the universe. Peter (1 Peter 5:19) and Paul (Ephesians 4:9) stated the same.

Some Gnostic manuscripts are quite similar to the Gospels' version of Jesus. A comparison of St John's Gospel with the Gnostic's Gospel of Truth reveals a compatibility of description regarding Jesus and his resurrected body that would deny any division of orthodox belief and heretical opinion. Yet the portrait of Jesus as the Christ is complicated and variously proposed in other texts.

The Apocalypse of James mentions a conversation between the resurrected Jesus and the grieving apostle James:

> Never have I experienced any kind of suffering, nor was I tormented. . . . [5]

In the Second Word of Seth, it is mentioned of Jesus:

> I did not suffer at all. They sought to punish me, and I died, but not in reality but only in appearance. . . . [6]

The Gnostic viewpoint sees Jesus as not truly suffering but yet giving the appearance that the torture and crucifixion were producing pain. In the Revelation of Peter, the savior states:

> He whom you see on the wood glad and laughing, this is the living Jesus. But he in whose hands and feet they drive nails is his fleshly likeness, it is the substitute. . . .
> Accordingly only that which is capable of suffering will suffer, in that the body is the substitute. He however who

was set free is my bodiless body; for I am only perceptible
spirit which is full of radiant light. . . . [7]

For the Gnostics, victory over the flesh means that Jesus transcended any pain. In so doing, he proves the liberation of the
spirit over matter and its deficiencies.

There is a curious story of St Teresa of Avila that relates
how once the convent nuns found her rapt in meditation and
attempted to revive her by sticking her with pins to no avail.
Likewise there are ancient techniques taught to yogis that enable
them to become immune to sensible pain while remaining
conscious of their environment.

The Unknown God

The ultimate Lord of Being is the unknown God. This God did
not create anything. The Gnostic concept of God is similar to
the Eastern notion of Brahman. There are no images or ideas
that can in any way describe this God. Genderless, God is real
but incomprehensible to the rational mind. By contrast with
sense and reason, God is unknown, yet the Father and Mother
of the All, the beginning and end of everything. Strange that
the best description of God is in negative terms. What God is
not is also the exact portrayal of God by Jewish and Christian
theologians and mystics. Thomas Aquinas, Meister Eckhart, the
author of *The Cloud of Unknowing*, John of the Cross, are but
a few authors whose experience, like that of many Eastern sages,
concurs with the Gnostic description. The revelation of gnosis
overcomes their fundamental ignorance.

The notion of addressing God as Father existed side by side
with revering God as a divine Mother. In the Gospel to the
Hebrews, Jesus speaks of "my Mother, the Spirit."[8] The same
is reiterated in the Gospel of Thomas and the Gospel of Philip.
There are many other manuscripts that describe the divinity as
feminine. Interestingly in the manuscript called *The Triple-
Formed Primal Thought*, the range of consciousness is predomi-

nantly identified as female and later asserts the androgynous dynamism of the human spirit. Here are echoes of tantra yoga with its description of consciousness as the primal powers of shakti (female) and siva (male).

Summary

The rediscovery of the hundreds of manuscripts that make up the *Nag Hammadi Library* have yet to be fully appreciated for their value as a form of Christianity and as a synthesis of spiritual traditions. The following reflections may be offered about the *Nag Hammadi Library*.

1. The context of the manuscripts is myth. There is no fixed dogma. The preference for myth allows for an absorption of various strands of diverse traditions that can explain the message. The wide differences and emphasis on just what is appropriate for each group of Gnostics can be tolerated within the multifaceted symbols comprising Gnostic mythology.
2. The Gnostics resisted idolizing any special teacher. The few Gnostic authors may have inspired followers but there is little evidence pointing to a cultic status for them as is found in other forms of Christianity around Jesus, Mary and the saints.

Unlike institutional Christians, the Gnostics did not share in the third-century movement that associated divine power on earth with a limited number of human agents – Apostles, martyrs, bishops and saints. Hence they resisted becoming consolidated into a clergy with its attendant policies and privileges. Their approach obviously alienated them from the more orthodox church.
3. There is a radical unknowability regarding God. While this strong position is not entirely absent from the Judaic-Christian Bible, it is rarely emphasized by orthodox theologians. The gods and traditions derived from the cosmos are entirely rejected as worthless. This disdain for the material world is more than just a recognition of the limitations of earthly existence; it shows

up in the manuscripts as a negative evaluation: matter is a perpetual enemy.

4. The emphasis upon self-redemption allows the Gnostics a wide diversity of beliefs that is evident in the *Nag Hammadi Library*. The central emphasis is on the practical truth of achieving liberation now, not a speculation about the cosmos or a discussion of the fine points of doctrine. Neither will faith produce liberation. One must be conscious of the real truth – the gnosis. The Gnostics saw themselves as the only true Christians. To be without gnosis is to remain in ignorance, like living in a nightmare. In the Dialogue of the Savior, when Jesus is asked to show Matthew the pure light and its place, Jesus replies, "Every one of you who has known himself has seen it."[9] Again in the Testimony of Truth we are told that one must become a "disciple of one's own mind."[10]

5. The worst evil that befalls people is self-ignorance, like a disease; the only cure is self-knowledge. In this Gnostic light the Gospels become favorable to the yoga insistence that self-knowledge is liberating. The Gnostic teacher Silvanus says: "Light the lamp within you."[11] The Gospel of Thomas likewise asserts: "When you come to know yourselves, then you will be known and you will realize that you are the sons of the living Father."[12]

In its complexity the Gnostic heritage offers to orthodox Christians the opportunity to reconsider the depth of spiritual experience available to seekers who follow Christ. As Christians ask questions about the meaning of life and inner experience that exceed the standard answers provided by institutional churches, the Gnostic writings, along with yogic practices, point to human horizons available for the exploration.

Notes

Chapter 1: *Traditions in Tandem*

1. Martyr, Justin. *Dialogue with Trypho*, (Baltimore; Westminster Press), 1958, p. 75.
2. Archbishop Jean Jadot in *Bulletin: Secretariatus pro Non-Christianis*, 1983, XVIII/1 52, p.22–23.

Chapter 2: *The Ways of Religious Consciousness*

1. van Ruysbroeck, Jan. *The Spiritual Espousals*, edited and translated by E. Colledge, (London: Sheed and Ward), 1952, p.187.
2. Meister Eckhart. *Sermon 99*. Quoted in Underhill, *Mysticism*, (New York: New American Library) 1955, p.420.
3. *Theologia Germanica*, ch. 41, quoted in Underhill, *op.cit.*, p. 418.
4. Underhill, *op. cit.*, p.342.
5. *Ibid.*, p.149.
6. Elmer, O'Brien. *Varieties of Mystic Experience*, (New York; New American Library), 1965, p.77.
7. *Ibid.*, p.79.
8. Maitri Upanishad, 6.17.
9. Mandaka Upanishad, 3.2.8.
10. Svetasvatara Upanishad, 2.15.
11. Kaivalya Upanishad, 7.
12. Katha Upanishad, 4.1.
13. *Ibid.*, 6. 18.
14. Richard of St Victor. *Selected Writings on Contemplation*, edited and translated by C. Kirchberger, (London: Sheed and Ward) 1957, p.203.
15. St Edmund Rich. "The Mirror" in: *The Mediaeval Mystics of England*, edited and translated by E. Colledge, (London: Sheed and Ward) 1961, p.137–39.

16. Origin. *Commentary on John 32.27* in: Andrew Louth, *Christian Mystical Tradition from Plato to Denys*, (Oxford: Oxford University Press) 1983, p.73.

17. Maslow, Abraham. *Religions, Values and Peak Experiences*, (New York: Viking Press), 1970, p.24–25.

18. *Ibid.*, p.25.

Chapter 5: *Yoga and The Jesus Prayer*

1. Kodloubovsky, E. and Palmer, G. E. H. (trs.). *Writings from the Philokalia on Prayer of the Heart*, (London: Faber and Faber), 1951, p.6.

2. The riddle of why Western Christianity lost this treasure of spirituality may be traced in some measure to the door of St Benedict. As the Father of Western Monasticism, he opened to his followers in Europe a path of spirituality based on the imitation of Christ as witnessed in his moral virtues. Without in any way minimizing the role of prayer or meditation in his rule, we see that there is not the slightest hint of the prayer of the heart nor any direction towards a psychophysical incorporation of these spiritual principles in his famous rule for the monastic life. As a monk of his time, Benedict was familiar with this ascetic approach, found both in the Rule of Basil, which he relied upon for the composition of his own rule, as well as in the Conferences of Cassian (360–435 A.D.). No doubt the Hesychast method was known to him. Whatever his reasons, he preferred not to introduce it in his writings nor apparently to his order of monks.

3. Kodloubovsky, E. and Palmer, G. E. H. *op. cit.*, p.192.

4. *Ibid.*, p.192–93.

5. The Yoga Sutras of Patanjali, 1.2–3.

6. Cuttat, Jacques-Albert. *The Encounter of Religions*, (New York: Desclie Company), 1960, p.102.

7. *Ibid.*, p.102.

8. *Ibid.*, p.103.

9. *Ibid.*, p.125.

10. Kodloubovsky, E. and Palmer, G. E. H., *op. cit.*, p.33.

11. Cuttat, *op. cit.*, p. 99.

12. Kodloubovsky, E. and Palmer, G. E. H., *cop. cit.*, p. 235.

13. Johnson, William (ed.), *The Cloud of Unknowing and the Book of*

the Privy Counseling (anon) (New York: Doubleday Image Books), 1973, p.149.

14. Ruysbroeck, John. *Adornment of the Spiritual Marriage,* translated by P. Wynschenk Dom, (London: Faber & Faber), 1916, 1.ii, ch. lxv.

15. Kavanaugh, Kieran and Rodriguez, Otilio (tr.). *The Collected Works of St John of the Cross,* (Washington D.C.:ICS Publications), 1964, p.152.

16. Kodloubovsky, E. and Palmer, G.E. H., *op. cit.,* p. 235.

Chapter 7: *The Meaning of Revelation*

1. Hollander, R. *Allegory in Dante's Commedia,* (Princeton: Princeton University Press) 1969, p.23+.

Chapter 10: *Miracles, Siddhis and Science*

1. Luther, Martin. "Sermons on the Gospel of St John" in *Luther's Works* edited by Jaroslav Pelikan, (St Louis: Concordia Publishers), 1955, chapters 14ff (24.367).

2. Calvin, John. *Institute of the Christian Religion,* translated by H. Beveridge, (Grand Rapids, Michigan: Eerdmans), 1953, IV.18, 2:636.

3. Barth, Karl. *Church Dogmatics,* edited and translated by G. W. Bromiley, T. F. Torrance, and others (Edinburgh: T. and T. Clark), 1936–69.

4. Bultmann, Rudolph. *Jesus Christ and Mythology,* (New York: C. Scribner's Sons), 1958, p.15.

5. Bultmann, Rudolph, et al. *Kerygma and Myth,* edited by H. Bartsch, revised edition of translation by R. H. Fuller, (New York: Harper & Row) 1961, p.4–5.

6. St Augustine, *City of God,* p.xxii.

7. Yoga Sutras of Patanjali, I.2,5.

8. *Ibid.,* II.21.

9. *Ibid.,* I.24.

10. The third pada of *The Yoga Sutras* outlines the range of control over the material realm available to the practitioner.

11. *The Yoga Sutras of Patanjali,* III.45.

12. Banerjee, S. *A Mystic Sage, Ma Anandamayi,* (Calcutta: S. Banerjee), 1973, p.82.

13. Ram Dass. *Miracle of Love, Stories about Neem Karoli Baba*, (New York: Dutton), 1979, p.47; 285.

14. Swami Rama, *Living with the Himalayan Masters*, (Honesdale, Pennsylvania: Himalayan Press), 1978, p.400–1.

15. See also the following works for a discussion of this concept: Bates, Charles in *Ransoming the Mind* (YES International); Brown, Barbara, *New Mind, New Body* (Harper & Row); Capra, Fritz, *The Tao of Physics* (Bantam); and Elmer and Alice Green, *Beyond Biofeedback* (Delta).

Chapter 11: *Christian Gnosticism and Yoga*

1. James Robinson (ed.). *The Nag Hammadi Library* (hereafter referred to as NHL), The Gospel of Truth, 13,22,1, (New York: Harper & Row) 1981.

2. The Gospel of Philip. II, 3, 75 NHL p.147.

3. Mundaka Upanishad II, 2, 10–11.

4. The Gospel of Philip, II, 3, 84, NHL.

5. Apocalypse of James V, 3, 31, 15–26, NHL.

6. Second Word of Seth VII, 2, 55, 9–56, NHL.

7. Revelation of Peter VII, 3, 81, 3, NHL.

8. Pagels, Elaine. *The Gnostic Gospels*, (New York: Vintage Books), Random House, 1981, p.62.

9. Dialogue of the Savior, III, 5, 132, NHL.

10. Testimony of Truth, IX, 3, 44, NHL.

11. The Teachings of Silvanus, VII, 4, 86, NHL.

12. The Gospel of Thomas, II, 2, 32, NHL.